Multilingual Learners in STEAM

Multilingual Learners in STEAM

Teaching Framework and Practical Tools for Elementary Grades

**Eun Kyung Ko
and Xiaoning Chen**

BLOOMSBURY ACADEMIC
NEW YORK • LONDON • OXFORD • NEW DELHI • SYDNEY

BLOOMSBURY ACADEMIC
Bloomsbury Publishing Inc, 1359 Broadway, New York, NY 10018, USA
Bloomsbury Publishing Plc, 50 Bedford Square, London, WC1B 3DP, UK
Bloomsbury Publishing Ireland, 29 Earlsfort Terrace, Dublin 2, D02 AY28, Ireland

BLOOMSBURY, BLOOMSBURY ACADEMIC and the Diana logo are
trademarks of Bloomsbury Publishing Plc

First published in the United States of America 2025

Cover design by Dustin Watson
Cover image © istock/nsta_photos

Library of Congress Cataloging-in-Publication Data is available

ISBN: HB: 978-1-5381-9747-9
          PB: 978-1-5381-9748-6
          ePub: 978-1-5381-9749-3
          ePDF: 979-8-7651-5494-6

Typeset by Integra Software Services Pvt. Ltd.
Printed and bound in the United States of America

For product safety related questions contact productsafety@bloomsbury.com.

To find out more about our authors and books visit www.bloomsbury.com
and sign up for our newsletters.

Contents

Acknowledgments

This book represents a culmination of our ongoing, collaborative work to promote equity in education and empower STEAM educators and multilingual learners. While we wrote the manuscript, many other people have contributed to its successful completion.

Dr. Eun Kyung Ko extends her deepest gratitude to her colleagues and contributors whose unwavering dedication, expertise, and insights have brought this book to fruition. She is especially grateful to her coauthor, Dr. Xiaoning Chen, for her invaluable expertise, dedication, and collaborative spirit, which enriched this work immeasurably. Together, we have strived to amplify the voices of multilingual learners, create culturally responsive teaching with linguistic justice, and foster opportunities for innovation and success in STEAM education.

Dr. Xiaoning Chen greatly appreciates her colleagues and students at National Louis University whose work inspires her to explore how visual literacy intersects with multiple content areas such as STEAM. It has been such a pleasure to work with the coauthor, Dr. Eun Kyung Ko, on this journey. Dr. Chen's deepest gratitude goes to Emeritus Professor Mark Newman, who has been a tremendous mentor and collaborator on visual literacy work.

Our appreciation also goes to the two chapter authors: Assistant Professor Vishodana Thamatharan and Professor Xiaoli Wen. Their expertise has significantly strengthened the scope and content of the book. We extend our heartfelt thanks to our colleague, Associate Professor Xue Han, for her invaluable contributions and expertise, which have greatly enriched the math component of STEAM in this book.

We would also like to express our sincere gratitude to the reviewers who provided valuable feedback on the book. Dr. Okhee Lee, Professor at New York University, Dr. Minjung Ryu, Associate Professor at University of Illinois Chicago, and Christy Smith, STEM teacher at Graves Elementary School in Illinois.

We would like to thank folks at Bloomsbury for their support, including Executive Acquisitions Editor Nathan Davidson and his assistant, Hollis Peterson, and Production Editor Chris Fischer and Charles Harmon in the book production process.

Last, Eun Kyung wishes to express her heartfelt thanks to her family for their steadfast encouragement and support. To her husband, Byoung Sug Kim, and her children, Enna and Juno, she is deeply grateful for their love, patience, and understanding, which have been her greatest sources of strength throughout this journey. Xiaoning would like to thank her family's continuous encouragement and support, especially her parents, Tiansheng and Lingling; her husband, Yuming; and son, Julian.

Companion Website

Visit https://www.bloomsburyonlineresources.com/multilingual-learners-in-steam

We provide this open-access website as a companion to this book to enhance your knowledge and practices of STEAM instruction for multilingual learners.

On the companion website, you will find the ESEM framework and additional resources related to each chapter. These resources include reflection questions, recommended activities, downloadable templates, relevant websites and readings.

Part I

Introduction and Framework

Introduction

This book is the result of collaborative efforts between two faculty members who share common scholarly interests on visual literacy but come from different disciplinary areas: STEAM and ESL/bilingual education. We intend to address three interrelated topics in this book. First, we focus on the content area of STEAM (science, technology, engineering, arts, and mathematics), aiming to illustrate why and how STEAM should be approached as an integrated discipline (NGSS Lead States, 2013), rather than a collection of separate subjects. Different terms that reflect the interdisciplinary learning approach exist (e.g., STREAM) in research and practice. When referencing literature, we keep the term in the original context as is. We adopt the term *STEAM* in this book as an integrated pedagogical framework for teaching and learning. *STEM* is also used to refer to a field of disciplines and careers that drives global innovation and employment opportunities.

Second, our targeted student population is young multilingual learners (MLs), who have rich cultural and linguistic resources and are in the process of acquiring English proficiency in the United States (see Figure I.1). There are many terms to describe this group of students, such as English learners (ELs), English language learners (ELLs), students with limited English proficiency, emergent bilinguals (EBs), and multilingual learners (MLs). ELs (or sometimes ELLs) is the official term used by federal and state agencies, policymakers, and researchers to refer to learners who are in the process of acquiring English proficiency. Other terms (e.g., EBs and MLs) positively shift the central focus from English, a deficit approach, to a much-needed asset-based perspective (Lee & Stephens, 2020; Moll et al., 1992; NASEM, 2018) where we value and embrace students' diverse home languages and cultures. In this book, we adopt the term *multilingual learners* (MLs) because we firmly believe that this term does justice to students' multilingual and multicultural resources. Further, the term is consistent with what was used in the updated 2020 WIDA (World-Class Instructional Design and Assessment) standards framework, which is adopted by 42 states, territories, and federal agencies in the United States and in schools worldwide. The terms used in research or data reports in reference to this group of students are kept intact. We acknowledge the challenges STEAM teachers encounter while working with MLs. At the same time, we intend to present a practical teaching framework and best practices that legitimize the significant role MLs' cultural and linguistic assets play in STEAM education.

Lastly, we address the intricate intersection where MLs converge with the STEAM content area through an equity and justice lens. This entails creating an inclusive learning environment when teaching STEAM, developing curricula that resonate with MLs' real-life interests and issues, and empowering MLs to activate their agency and promote social justice. The concepts of STEAM and MLs will be discussed in more detail in Chapter 1.

Figure I.1 STEAM Learning with Diverse Students. SDI Productions (2016), istockphoto.com.

What Are the Challenges STEAM Teachers Face?

Given the unique characteristics of MLs and the current status of STEAM education, teachers face many challenges. One of these challenges relates to an equity-centered and practical teaching framework. In their systematic literature review of equity-oriented STEM (and STEAM) education frameworks, Jackson et al. (2021) found that there was no existing conceptual STEAM literacy framework that explicitly centered on equity. Without an equity-centered framework, teachers may struggle with creating an equitable learning community and STEAM curriculum where diverse cultural and linguistic resources are viewed as assets instead of deficits. Moreover, many theoretical frameworks in education remain abstract, leaving teachers unsure of how to apply them in real classrooms (Reider et al., 2021; Shillingford et al., 2017). A related challenge is for STEAM teachers to develop inclusive ideologies (Lemmi et al., 2019) and implement justice-focused pedagogical approaches (Davis & Bautista, 2024) that provide affordances to MLs' content and language learning. Further, as the world becomes more interconnected, students need to develop skills to navigate different cultures and collaborate across disciplines (Chine & Larwin, 2022; Guzey et al., 2017). Teachers are challenged to keep their pedagogies up-to-date and effective in a rapidly evolving educational landscape and develop strategies to enhance students' global and cross-disciplinary competence.

How Does This Book Contribute to Providing Solutions to the Challenges?

This book contributes to the field of STEAM education by supporting pre- and in-service teachers to address the abovementioned challenges. It enhances STEAM teachers' understanding and use of an equitable teaching framework (i.e., the Equitable STEAM Education for Multilingual

Learners [ESEM] Framework featured in Chapter 2) and practical tools within diverse classrooms and beyond.

Specifically, this book has a dedicated focus on how to apply an equity and justice-focused framework to enhance the integrated MLs' language and STEAM learning in elementary grades. Our understanding of equity and justice draws from Gutiérrez (2009) and Jackson et al. (2021). Key components of equity include *access* and *opportunity*, which ensure the removal of obstacles for all students to participate in integrated STEAM learning experiences. Moreover, equity encompasses the components of *identity* and *power*, which connects well with the concept of justice. It is essential that students see themselves as valuable members of the STEAM learning community. Further, they are empowered to activate their agency and use what they learn to promote positive changes in the world. "In essence, each and every student needs access to high-quality STEM learning experiences that affirm their identities as important members of the STEM community who are working to make the world a better place" (Jackson et al., 2021, p. 5).

At the core of our approach is an equity and justice-focused framework that synthesizes key research and theories such as linguistically responsive teaching (Lucas & Villegas, 2010), translanguaging (García et al., 2017), and critical visual literacy (Chung, 2013) to enrich culturally responsive pedagogy (Hammond, 2014). Further, to provide a real-world context, this book employs templates and examples based on class profiles, which serve as a guide for teachers as they navigate the realm of justice-focused STEAM education. The curriculum and classroom activities are based on MLs' everyday lives and help bridge their daily language use to academic language demands. Packed with practical examples and actionable recommendations, it offers a comprehensive tool kit for engaging with MLs and larger communities.

Moreover, the focal point of the book revolves around the intersectionality of diversity, equity, and inclusion. The book addresses a critical need for teachers to effectively engage and empower young MLs in STEAM education. On the one hand, MLs are confronted with the dual challenge of developing English proficiency and STEAM content mastery. On the other hand, the average STEAM curriculum is not necessarily designed in a way that is equitable and justice-focused or that allows MLs to bring in their cultural and linguistic assets to enrich the learning experience and promote social change for equity. Teachers are often not provided with relevant resources and teaching methods (Margolis et al., 2010; NCSES, 2023; Vakil, 2018) that enable them to effectively address this need. Through the framework of this book, we aim to support teachers to inspire and empower MLs to continue pursuing STEAM as a future profession and to become agents in transformative changes toward social justice.

Two additional features make this book especially relevant to STEAM teachers. One feature is the inclusion of examples based on class profiles that illustrate how the framework can be used in practice. These examples are helpful for pre-service teachers to understand the real classroom situation better and for in-service teachers to select and design specific strategies for incorporating culture and language into their STEAM teaching. In addition, this book provides STEAM teaching resources and templates for teachers to validate and embrace cultural and linguistic diversity.

In summary, this book focuses on the theme of diversity, equity, and inclusion in STEAM education, particularly as they intersect with the content and language development of MLs. It features an integrated approach to STEAM education, effective teaching strategies, and justice-focused curriculum in the multilingual and multicultural teaching context. It aims to support teachers to strive for a more inclusive and equitable STEAM education.

How Is the Book Organized?

This book is organized such that each part builds on the preceding one to promote diversity, equity, and inclusion in STEAM education. There are a total of three parts. Part I sets the stage of the book's content and introduces the ESEM Framework that guides the subsequent chapters found in part II.

Chapter 1 helps educators develop an understanding of the heterogeneity of MLs present in today's classrooms. It also serves to contextualize the integrated STEAM approach and delves into the impact of culture and language on students' learning. Finally, it provides insights into how teachers can enhance engagement and enrich MLs' STEAM learning experience.

Chapter 2 introduces the ESEM Framework, weaving together components from culturally and linguistically responsive teaching

(Hammond, 2014; Lucas & Villegas, 2010), translanguaging (García et al., 2017), and critical visual literacy (Chung, 2013). This framework serves as a guide for teachers to develop and implement an approach that promotes inclusive and equitable STEAM teaching and learning.

Part II is the application section. It takes the framework and empowers readers with the know-how to implement it across various aspects of STEAM education. Each chapter in part II focuses on distinct dimensions of this transformative educational framework. The reader follows a detailed journey through the practical implementation of the suggested ESEM framework for culturally and linguistically inclusive STEAM education. Chapters 3 to 8 form a comprehensive guide to implementing the ESEM framework in diverse educational settings.

Chapter 3 explores the concept of the STEAM learning community and its connection with the core principles in the ESEM framework. Further, we offer three practical tools to establish an inclusive STEAM learning community.

Chapter 4 guides teachers in crafting curriculum and evaluating student progress while incorporating cultural and linguistic aspects. The class profile provides a real-world context, and the chapter offers curriculum and assessment examples and templates for different age groups.

Chapter 5 focuses on designing engaging classroom instruction aligned with language development (i.e., WIDA) and STEAM education (i.e., NGSS) standards. It models how to enact the core principles and key teaching practices in the ESEM framework by designing engaging STEAM activities with differentiation and support strategies for MLs. The chapter provides practical classroom examples and templates suitable for various grade levels.

Chapter 6 explores collaborative elements within the ESEM framework. It emphasizes building strong partnerships with families and communities to enhance STEAM education. Strategies for meaningful engagement are presented through classroom examples, and templates are provided for educators to foster connections beyond the classroom.

Chapter 7 delves into selecting and integrating technology into the classroom. It shows how to leverage technology within and outside the classroom to enrich STEAM teaching and learning. Classroom examples showcase technology's applications and challenges. The chapter also provides templates spanning different age groups, facilitating seamless technology integration.

Chapter 8 highlights continuous professional development, collaboration, and advocacy within the ESEM framework. It provides resources to enhance STEAM education knowledge and skills for MLs and advocates for students' needs. A vignette prompts reflection within a school community, promoting an environment of growth and improvement. Table I.1 shows the featured class profiles and STEAM examples for each chapter.

Part III comprises a conclusion that summarizes the content and insights shared. With practical class profiles, tangible examples, and meaningful insights, educators will be equipped to create a culturally and linguistically inclusive STEAM learning environment, grow professionally, and champion the needs of MLs.

Finally, the companion website for this book provides a plethora of additional resources such as detailed lesson plans, recommended children's book lists, STEAM-related activity resources, and PD and funding opportunities.

Table I.1 Overview of Class Profiles and Examples in Selected Chapters

Chapters	Class Profiles	Showcased STEAM Examples
2. ESEM framework	2 (Mr. Gilbert & Ms. Fang, 3rd, suburban, CA)	Severe weather & rain gear (Earth science +Engineering practice)
3. Learning community	1 (Ms.Young, 1st, inner city, Chicago, IL)	Bird migration (Life science + Community issue)
4. Curriculum	3 (Ms.Nowak, 5th, rural, IL)	Eco-friendly agricultural community (Physical science + Community impact)
5. Instruction	2 (Mr. Gilbert & Ms. Fang, 3rd, suburban, CA)	Oil spill (Physical science + Mathematics)
6. Family and community partnership	1 (Ms.Young, 1st, inner city, Chicago, IL)	Community garden (Environmental Science + Community partnership)
7. Technology	3 (Ms.Nowak, 5th, rural, IL)	Butterfly migration (Life Science + Community engagement)
8. PD, collaboration, and advocacy	2 (Mr. Gilbert & Ms. Fang, 3rd, suburban, CA)	Earthquake (Earth science + Technology integration)

References

Chine, D., & Larwin, K. (2022). The impact of STEM integration on student achievement using HLM: A case study. *Journal of Research in STEM Education, 8*(1), 1–23.

Chung, S. K. (2013). Critical visual literacy. *International Journal of Arts Education, 11*(2), 1–21.

Davis, E. A., & Bautista, J. (2024, January). *Preservice teachers' lesson planning for justice-oriented elementary science* [Conference paper]. Association for Science Teacher Education Conference, New Orleans, LA, United States.

García, O., Johnson, S. I., & Seltzer, K. (2017). *The translanguaging classroom.* Caslon.

Gutiérrez, R. (2009). Embracing the inherent tensions in teaching mathematics from an equity stance. *Democracy in Education, 18*(3), 9–15.

Guzey, S., Harwell, M., Moreno, M., Peralta, Y., & Moore, T. (2017). The impact of design-based STEM integration curricula on student achievement in engineering, science, and mathematics. *Journal of Science Education and Technology, 26*, 207–222.

Hammond, Z. (2014). *Culturally responsive teaching and the brain: Promoting authentic engagement and rigor among culturally and linguistically diverse students.* Corwin.

Jackson, C., Mohr-Schroeder, M. J., Bush, S. B., Maiorca, C., Roberts, T., Yost, C., & Fowler, A. (2021). Equity-oriented conceptual framework for K-12 STEM literacy. *International Journal of STEM Education, 8*, 38. https://doi.org/10.1186/s40594-021-00294-z

Lee, O., & Stephens, A. (2020). English learners in STEM subjects: Contemporary views on STEM subjects and language with English learners. *Educational Researcher, 49*(6), 426–432. DOI:10.3102/001318 9X20923708

Lemmi, C., Brown, B. A., Wild, A., Zummo, L., & Sedlacek, Q. (2019). Language ideologies in science education. *Science Teacher Education, 4*, 854–874. https://doi.org/10.1002/sce.21508

Lucas, T., & Villegas, A. M. (2010). The missing piece in teacher education: The preparation of linguistically responsive teachers. *National Society for the Study of Education, 109*, 297–318.

Margolis, J., Estrella, R., Goode, J., Holme, J., & Nao, K. (2010). *Stuck in the shallow end: Education, race, and computing.* MIT Press.

Moll, L., Amanti, C., Neff, D., & Gonzalez, N. (1992). Funds of knowledge for teaching: Using a qualitative approach to connect homes to classrooms. *Theory into Practice, 31*(2), 132–141.

National Academies of Sciences, Engineering, and Medicine (NASEM). (2018). *English learners in STEM subjects: Transforming classrooms, schools, and lives.* National Academies Press.

National Center for Educational Statistics. (2023). *English learners in public schools.* U.S. Department of Education, Institute of Education Sciences. https://nces.ed.gov/programs/coe/indicator/cgf

National Center for Science and Engineering Statistics (NCSES). (2023). *Diversity and STEM: Women, minorities, and persons with disabilities 2023* [Special report]. National Science Foundation, NSF 23-315. https://ncses.nsf.gov/pubs/nsf23315/

NGSS Lead States. (2013). *Next Generation Science Standards: For states, by states.* National Academies Press.

Reider, D., Davis, N., & Nariman, N. (2021). *Problem-based learning increases STEM interest for high school students and instructors* [Conference presentation]. IAFOR International Conference on Education, Honolulu, HI, United States.

Shillingford, A., Oh, S., & Finnell, L. (2017). Promoting STEM career development among students and parents of color: Are school counselors leading the charge? *Professional School Counseling, 21*(1b), 1–11.

Vakil, S. (2018). Ethics, identity, and political vision: Toward a justice-centered approach to equity in computer science education. *Harvard Educational Review, 88*(1), 26–52.

WIDA. (2020). *English Language Development (ELD) Standards Framework, 2020 edition: Kindergarten-grade 12.* Board of the University of Wisconsin System. https://wida.wisc.edu/teach/standards/eld

1

Multilingual Learners in STEAM

Ms. Nowak is a fifth-grade teacher in a rural community school. Out of the 20 students in her classroom, eight speak a language other than English at home. These students come from families with diverse cultural and linguistic backgrounds, and their home languages include Spanish, Portuguese, Polish, and Vietnamese. Ms. Nowak's classroom profile provides a glimpse into the rich tapestry of diversity that characterizes today's educational landscape.

Who Are Multilingual Learners?

To answer the question of who MLs are, we need to explore factors that play a role in shaping various aspects of their identities. Statistically speaking, the percentage of US public school students who were identified as ELs increased from fall 2010, standing at 9.2 percent, or 4.5 million students, to fall 2020, reaching 10.3 percent, or 5.0 million students (NCES, 2023). Upon examining the pattern across different grade levels, it shows that a higher proportion of public school students in the elementary grades were categorized as ELs than their counterparts in the secondary levels (fall 2020 data, NCES, 2023). For instance, 12.9 percent of kindergarteners were classified as ELs. In comparison, only 5.6 percent of 12th graders fell under the same category (NCES, 2023). This pattern highlights the crucial role of the early school years in MLs' journey toward attaining English language proficiency.

In contrast to the common misconception that most of these students are foreign born, the majority (72%) of ELs in US public schools were born in the United States (Bialik et al., 2018). While a significant proportion of ELs have Hispanic backgrounds, there are variations in the racial and ethnic compositions among this group. Following Hispanic (77.1%), the next three racial and ethnic backgrounds of ELs in fall 2020 were Asian (10.2%), White (6.3%), and Black (4.3%) (NCES, 2023).

The most commonly reported EL home language is Spanish, which represents 3.7 million, or 75.5% of all ELs and 7.8% of all public school students in fall 2020 (NCES, 2023). The next four most commonly reported home languages other than English were Arabic, Chinese, Vietnamese, and Portuguese (NCES, 2023). Portuguese is the home language representing the most significant change, with the total number of students nearly tripled from fall 2009 to fall 2020 (NCES, 2023).

In addition, 16.1% of ELs were dually identified with disabilities (fall 2020 data, NCES, 2023). We recognize that this is an important group of learners with unique needs and challenges, but it is out of the scope of this book to address their academic experiences.

The varied racial and ethnic backgrounds of MLs are intricately connected to their families' socioeconomic status (SES). Quintero and Hansen (2021) pointed out that ELs continue to experience economic segregation in the United States, as the majority (75%) attend 20% of the schools. Those schools typically serve high-poverty communities. Within this group of ELs, approximately 37% are from households with a low SES, and 54% have parents with limited to no educational background (Quintero & Hansen, 2021). Korhonen's (2023) research shows that more than 30% of children below the poverty threshold spoke a language other than English at home in 2019. In contrast, among the children above the poverty threshold, about 20% did not speak English at home.

Further, urban schools have a considerably higher percentage of students experiencing high poverty levels when compared with their suburban and rural counterparts (NCES, 2023). EL enrollment was higher in urban school districts (13.7%) than those in suburban (10%) and rural (4.4%) areas (fall 2020 data, NCES, 2023). Hispanic students exhibited the highest percentage (38%) in US high-poverty schools, while White students were the lowest (7%) (fall 2021 data, NCES, 2023).

Language Program Models Serving Multilingual Learners

Due to the heterogeneous nature of MLs, several categories are created to identify the unique needs of these students in the school setting. First, newcomers are students who were born outside of the country and recently moved to the United States with no or very limited English proficiency (US Department of Education, 2016). Second, SIFE refers to students with interrupted or limited formal education due to reasons such as warfare or poverty prior to their start of schooling in the United States. Third and last, the term L-TELs represents long-term ELs who, despite receiving English language support services in US schools for at least six years, have not met the reclassification criteria.

Different language program models are available to serve MLs' linguistic and academic needs. These models can be generally categorized into three groups based on the choice of the instructional language(s) for content learning (NASEM, 2018). The first type is to use primary language instruction for newcomers. This aims to support students in continuing their cognitive and academic development using their primary language while they begin to learn a new language. The second type falls under bilingual language instruction, where the primary language is used as a bridge to transition to English. One of these programs is the transitional bilingual model, where the ratio of primary language reduces while that of English increases as time progresses. Most of these programs transition students to a 100% English environment by the upper elementary grades. Another bilingual program model is the dual language program, where both the primary and target languages are used throughout the program with the goal of helping students become bilingual and biliterate. The third type is English-only instruction. Some examples include English as a second language (ESL), content-based ESL, or sheltered instruction. Despite their variations, all language program models, mandated by law to primarily focus on English language development, are frequently not structured in a manner that allows ELs to sustain and enhance age-appropriate knowledge of STEM subjects (NASEM, 2018). Furthermore, there is less priority given to assessing STEM-related outcomes (NASEM, 2018).

Meeting Multilingual Students Through Their Diverse Cultural and Linguistic Profiles

To move beyond the numbers and provide a more detailed description of the MLs in US elementary schools, we present three different class profiles (see Table 1.1). We intentionally created these class profiles to show the distinctive characteristics of MLs in various language program models at different geographic locations. These class profiles and the representative MLs will be referenced throughout the book to vividly illustrate best practices that enhance STEAM teaching and learning.

In the section above, we contextualize the changing educational landscape with the increasing number of MLs from a variety of linguistic, cultural, racial, ethnic, and socioeconomic backgrounds in US schools. As teachers in a classroom, it is critical to get to know the MLs so we can leverage their rich assets and address their unique challenges. In the following, we will elaborate on why we focus on STEAM (science, technology, engineering, arts, and mathematics) education and what integrated STEAM education means to MLs at elementary schools.

Table 1.1 Multilingual Class Profiles

Class Profiles			
Profile Number	1	2	3
Grade/ Setting	1st grade in an urban inner-city, high-poverty community	3rd grade in a suburban community	5th grade in a rural community
English Language Program	Transitional bilingual program (Spanish and English)	ESL pull-out and push-in program	Content-based language instruction program

Sample ML Students	*Jose:* Born in the US to first-generation immigrant parents from Mexico; speaks Spanish and English. *Lyla:* Born in the US to first-generation Arab American parents; speaks Arabic, English, and Spanish.	*Olha:* A newcomer who was born in Ukraine but moved with her family to the US six months ago; speaks Ukrainian and English. *Lin:* Born in Australia to Chinese parents and moved back to China. The family immigrated to the US one year ago. Lin speaks Mandarin Chinese and English.	*Allin:* Born in Angola with Umbundu- and Portuguese-speaking parents. Allin is at risk of becoming a long-term English learner (L-TEL). Allin speaks Umbundu, Portuguese, and English. *Mario:* Considered a student with interrupted or limited formal education (SIFE). He was born in Venezuela and had interrupted schooling while the family fled political turmoil and economic collapse before immigrating to the US. Mario speaks Spanish and English.

Why Do We Focus on STEAM Education?

The problems we encounter today are often intricate and multifaceted, extending beyond the boundaries of individual disciplines. To effectively address these real-world issues, there is a growing need for the integration of concepts and skills from multiple disciplines (Roehrig et al., 2021).

The Next Generation Science Standards (NGSS) provides a framework for K–12 science education in the United States (Reiser, 2012), aiming to prepare students for the challenges of the 21st century. Based on NGSS (NGSS Lead States, 2013), STEM encompasses an interdisciplinary educational approach that integrates science, technology, engineering, and mathematics to promote deeper understanding, critical thinking, and practical problem-solving skills.

The reason we adopt STEAM in this book is because the letter *A* represents arts, which is closely connected to STEM in terms of multimodality and visual literacy. Our communication in everyday life and education has become increasingly multimodal. For example, the bulletin board in a park has an infographic using print, pictures, and graphics to show all the wild animals and plants that adapt to the habitat of the area. Digital textbooks, in addition to using the modes of print and visuals, are able to incorporate hyperlinks to multimedia resources such as audio and videos. Multimodality, including linguistic and other semiotic modes, provides new affordances for learners to access the core curriculum and communicate learning (NASEM, 2018).

The visual is one of the key modes in multimodality. Visual literacy refers to a set of skills learners need to view, make sense of, analyze, and interpret visuals and create visual representations to express meaning (Avgerinou & Pettersson, 2011). These visual literacy skills need to be explicitly taught in a scaffolded approach and frequently practiced (Avgerinou, 2001; Chen & Newman, 2022). In STEAM education, students apply visual literacy skills when they view and analyze visuals such as photos, maps, and data charts, synthesizing information to formulate evidence-supported claims. They then generate multimodal representations to showcase their learning.

Given the increasingly multimodal nature of communication, WIDA (2020) expands the modes of communication from four language domains (i.e., listening, speaking, reading, and writing) to the interpretive and expressive domains accordingly (see Figure 1.1). The interpretive domain now includes listening, reading, and *viewing*. Similarly, the expressive domain encompasses speaking, writing, and *representing*. These two additions are particularly relevant to visual literacy.

The core principles of STEAM education are grounded in the idea that STEM and the arts are more effective and pertinent when taught collaboratively rather than in isolation (Quigley & Herro, 2016). STEAM education offers enhanced opportunities for effective collaboration

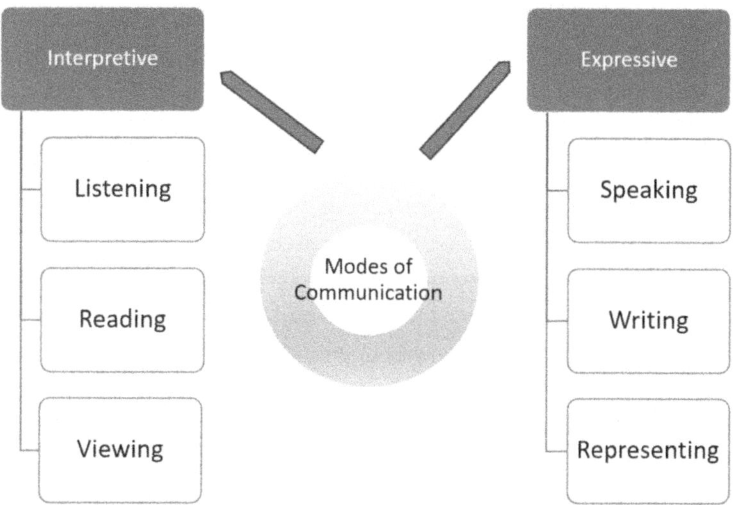

Figure 1.1 Modes of Communication. Author adapted from WIDA (2020) Standards Framework, https://wida.wisc.edu/teach/standards/eld/2020

among students throughout the learning process (Herro et al., 2018). It also provides more chances to promote student creativity and social empowerment (Allina, 2017). With the integration of multimodality and visual literacy, STEAM education offers diverse opportunities for MLs to express their creativity without the limitations imposed by language barriers. This integration has proven to be transformative, going beyond the mere generation of new content knowledge.

In actual scientific research and technological development, boundaries among the disciples are blurred. Here is an example of renewable energy and sustainability to explain the need for integrating multiple disciplines within STEAM education at the elementary level.

Scenario: Imagine a town named Greenville that wants to switch to using more renewable energy sources, like solar and wind power, to reduce its impact on the environment and ensure a cleaner future.

- *Science (Physical Science):* Students need to learn about solar energy, how solar panels work, and how wind energy is generated. They explore basic concepts, like light, shadow, and the movement of air, to help them understand the sources of renewable energy.

- *Technology:* Using online tools or simple solar energy sensors, students collect real-time data on solar energy generation in different countries. They learn how to operate basic data collection devices and how to analyze the collected data.
- *Engineering:* Students explore simple models of solar panels and wind turbines, fostering creativity and understanding basic engineering concepts. They may also learn about energy-efficient appliances.
- *Arts:* Students demonstrate their comprehension of renewable energy by engaging in creative activities, including artistic interpretation of distribution of solar panels and wind turbines across the nation and, developing visual representations highlighting the advantages of clean energy.
- *Mathematics:* Students engage in activities that involve measuring sunlight and wind speed. They learn to calculate how much energy can be generated from solar panels and wind turbines, fostering practical math skills.
- *Environmental Science*: Students discuss the importance of reducing pollution and conserving natural resources. They learn about the effects of fossil fuels on the environment and how using renewable energy sources can help.

By integrating these disciplines, elementary school students develop a well-rounded understanding of renewable energy and sustainability. They connect abstract concepts with real-world applications, fostering curiosity and critical thinking. This multidisciplinary approach nurtures a holistic view of how STEAM and other subjects work together to address complex issues like environmental sustainability. Moreover, it makes learning enjoyable and relatable, and empowers young learners to become environmentally conscious citizens who can contribute to a better world.

In summary, the inclusion of arts in STEM, forming STEAM, mirrors the interconnectedness of real scientific research and technology development, providing a more accurate representation of how these fields interact in professional settings. It not only enhances the overall educational experience but also contributes to breaking down barriers that may have hindered the involvement of certain communities in the STEM disciplines. This holistic approach recognizes the value of creativity and diverse perspectives, fostering a more inclusive and innovative learning environment.

What Does Integrated STEAM Education Mean in Elementary Grades?

Incorporating STEAM principles into education is crucial for several reasons. First, integrated education nurtures critical thinking and problem-solving skills by encouraging students to analyze complex challenges from multiple perspectives and develop diverse innovative solutions (Erduran, 2020; Takeuchi et al., 2020). This cultivates a mindset of inquiry and adaptability, essential for navigating the complexities of the 21st century. For example, when MLs delve into complex phenomena such as renewable energy and sustainability, their linguistic and cultural backgrounds empower them to ask insightful and critical questions and might propose a different approach to solving the issues.

Second, STEAM education promotes hands-on, experiential learning, allowing students to apply abstract concepts to real-world scenarios. This bridges the gap between abstract knowledge and practical application, enhancing students' meaningful learning experiences (English, 2016; Simoncini & Lasen, 2018). MLs, in particular, can enhance their learning experience by engaging in hands-on STEAM activities. This approach enables them to expand beyond emerging English proficiency, fostering a more comprehensive grasp of subject matter knowledge pertaining to renewable energy and sustainability. Moreover, with a deeper comprehension of the context, MLs can more readily translate their learning into actionable steps.

Therefore, STEAM education fosters inclusivity and diversity by encouraging students from various backgrounds to engage in problem solving and exploration (Chen & Lin, 2019; Jackson et al., 2021; Li et al., 2020). It transcends cultural and linguistic barriers, nurturing a collaborative learning environment that reflects the interconnected nature of our world. Ultimately, STEAM education equips students with the tools to become informed, engaged citizens capable of making evidence-based decisions and contributing positively to their communities (Hacıoğlu & Gülhan, 2021; Tytler, 2020).

How Do Culture and Language Intersect With MLs' STEAM Learning?

Culture plays a significant role in shaping the way people think, talk, and interact with the world around them. It is a multifaceted construct that encompasses various aspects and components. Hall (1976) proposed the cultural iceberg model, where he compared the external, conscious aspects of culture, such as cultural products and practices, as the tip of the iceberg. These aspects of culture can be explicitly learned and easily changed. However, the internal, subconscious aspects of culture are largely hidden beneath the surface, which include beliefs, perspectives, and values that underlie practices and products. These aspects of culture are implicitly learned and difficult to change. The implication of Hall's (1976) cultural iceberg model for teachers is that we have to move beyond the superficial aspects of culture to develop a deeper and sophisticated understanding of MLs' cultures.

Culture is also dynamic. In the early years, young children are largely immersed in their home culture. They learn from their primary caregivers how to talk and behave, what the value systems are, and why they are important. As they start to interact more with people in other sociocultural settings, like schools, children have the opportunity to adapt their cultural knowledge and cultivate competence in cross-cultural communication. MLs regularly crossing cultural boundaries undergo a similar process in refining and enhancing their cultural knowledge and competence.

Language is a critical component of culture. Vygotsky (1978) views language as the medium of culture. It reflects and shapes people's perspectives of the world, as well as their interaction patterns. For instance, the Chinese idiom "光阴似箭" translates to "Time flies like an arrow" in English, illustrating the significance of time in Chinese culture. The seminal study by Heath (1983) found that children's communication and interaction patterns differ significantly across cultural groups, with variations based on race and socioeconomic status. Along the same line, Fillmore's (2000) study suggested that children from diverse cultural and language backgrounds often experience disconnected patterns of communication and interaction between home and school. Consequently, they are often placed in a disadvantageous position when acquiring foundational skills, such as how to interact with others and communicate for academic learning (Fillmore, 2000).

Halliday (1975) proposed that language is more than a means to communicating with others; rather, language is a cultural code that serves the function of socializing children to be members of a society. Therefore, language is functional, and the way we communicate with others depends on the features of sociocultural contexts (Halliday, 1975). A key concept in Halliday's functional language model is register, defined as "a variety of language, corresponding to a variety of situations" (Halliday & Hasan, 1985, p. 38). For example, the register of children's playground communication varies significantly from the specialized register for STEAM learning in the classroom due to different contextual features, such as who we are speaking to, what the communication topic is, and how language and other semiotic modes are used. The implication of understanding language in the sense of register is that the discipline-specific demands on students in STEAM classrooms should extend beyond vocabulary as the sole focus, incorporating the dimensions of language at the sentence and discourse levels (NASEM, 2018).

The theoretical perspective that views language as functional (Halliday, 1975) has shaped contemporary views on language development in disciplinary content, which is reflected in the WIDA (2020) English language development (ELD) standards framework for MLs. The WIDA Science Standard 4 description (2020), for instance, has changed from "language *of* science" to "language *for* science," suggesting that the focus of language development is on "what language does" (Grapin et al., 2019) in the discipline of science.

A similar shift has taken place in STEAM subjects. Instead of focusing on mastering a set of content knowledge and skills, contemporary views place a strong emphasis on "knowledge-in-use" (Lee & Stephens, 2020). That is, students engage in authentic disciplinary practices in STEAM classrooms, in which they use knowledge and skills to make sense of phenomena, construct claims, argue with evidence, and develop models to solve problems.

The 2018 report from the National Academies of Sciences, Engineering, and Medicine (NASEM) highlights the relationship between language and STEM: "Language is a product of doing science, not a precursor or prerequisite for doing science and ELs need ample opportunities to do science" (p. 65). It is through engaging in disciplinary practices in the classroom that mirror the practices of STEM professionals in the real world that MLs develop disciplinary content and learn to communicate disciplinary meaning (NASEM, 2018).

In summary, this section emphasizes the interconnected relationship of culture and language in the context of MLs' STEAM learning. Culture is complex and dynamic, particularly when we examine MLs' understanding of who they are as they cross cultural boundaries. To support their identity development as STEAM learners, it is essential for MLs to engage in authentic, interdisciplinary practices and use language in meaningful ways. Such opportunities enable "these learners to bring their full range of knowledge and resources to learning and to realize their full potential" (NASEM, 2018, p. 33).

What Are the Standards That Guide STEAM Education for MLs?

In addition to the Common Core State Standards (CCSS) for math (2010), there are three key sets of standards that provide guidelines for working with MLs in STEAM education: NGSS (Next Generation Science Standards, https://www.nextgenscience.org/), WIDA English Language Development (ELD) Standards (https://wida.wisc.edu/teach/standards/eld), and NCAS (National Core Arts Standards, https://www.nationalartsstandards.org/). NGSS and NCAS outline the STEAM content, or what to learn at different grade levels, while WIDA provides support that allows MLs to use language for disciplinary purposes. We will provide a brief overview of each of these standards and discuss the connection between them.

NGSS is a comprehensive framework for K–12 science education in the United States, designed to integrate seamlessly with STEAM initiatives. NGSS emphasizes a holistic approach to science learning, incorporating disciplinary core ideas (DCI), crosscutting concepts (XCC), and science and engineering practices (SEP). These three dimensions are expected to be taught through each standard, and they guide teachers in designing experiences that foster deeper understanding, critical thinking, and real-world application of science principles.

Through hands-on exploration and inquiry-based learning, NGSS aims to cultivate a diverse, skilled workforce capable of addressing the complex challenges of the 21st century. In addition to the three dimensions, NGSS also includes grade bands, which specify the expected proficiency levels for students at different grade levels (K–2, 3–5, 6–8, and 9–12). Each grade band contains performance expectations that outline what students should know and be able to do at each stage of their education. By organizing standards into grade bands, NGSS provides a clear progression of learning across the K–12 continuum, ensuring that students build on their understanding of STEAM concepts and practices as they advance through school.

NCAS (2014) play a critical role in STEAM education by emphasizing the integration of artistic processes and concepts with science, technology, engineering, and mathematics. These standards provide a framework for engaging students in the creative and innovative aspects of learning, encouraging them to approach challenges with artistic problem-solving and design thinking. By highlighting processes such as creating, performing, responding, and connecting (see Table 1.2.), NCAS enables MLs to explore and express their understanding of STEAM concepts through diverse mediums like visual art, music, theater, and digital media. This multimodal engagement is particularly beneficial for MLs, as it allows them to communicate ideas and demonstrate learning beyond traditional language-heavy assessments, supporting equity and inclusion in STEAM education.

WIDA is a US-based organization committed to advancing the field of language development (WIDA, 2024). It achieves this goal through developing a research-based ELD framework, establishing language standards and corresponding assessments, and providing resources and professional development for teachers (WIDA, 2024). The WIDA 2020 edition demonstrates "the belief that multilingual learners are best served when they learn content and language together in linguistically and culturally sustaining ways" (p. 4). It is grounded in four big ideas, which are (1) equity of opportunity and access; (2) integration of content and language; (3) collaboration among stakeholders; and (4) a functional approach to language development. In line with these big ideas, WIDA (2020) presents the following five ELD standards:

- ELD Standard 1: Language for Social and Instructional Purposes
- ELD Standard 2: Language for Language Arts
- ELD Standard 3: Language for Mathematics
- ELD Standard 4: Language for Science
- ELD Standard 5: Language for Social Studies

Table 1.2 National Core Arts Standards (2014)

Artistic Processes	Creating	Performing/Presenting/Producing	Responding	Connecting
	Definition: Conceiving and developing new artistic ideas and work.	Definitions: • Performing: Realizing artistic ideas and work through interpretation and presentation. • Presenting: Interpreting and sharing artistic work. • Producing: Realizing and presenting artistic ideas and work.	Definition: Understanding and evaluating how the arts convey meaning.	Definition: Relating artistic ideas and work with personal meaning and external context.
Anchor Standards	Students will • Generate and conceptualize artistic ideas and work. • Organize and develop artistic ideas and work. • Refine and complete artistic work.	Students will • Select, analyze, and interpret artistic work for presentation. • Develop and refine artistic techniques and work for presentation. • Convey meaning through the presentation of artistic work.	Students will • Perceive and analyze artistic work. • Interpret intent and meaning in artistic work. • Apply criteria to evaluate artistic work.	Students will • Synthesize and relate knowledge and personal experiences to make art. • Relate artistic ideas and works with societal, cultural, and historical context to deepen understanding.

In the context of this book, ELD standards 3 and 4 are the most relevant, in addition to standard 1. These standards highlight language functions not only pertinent to specific disciplines but also spanning across all areas of schooling. Further, resource materials are grouped by grade-level clusters of K, 1, 2–3, 4–5, 6–8, and 9–12.

The WIDA ELD Standards Framework (2020) consists of four components: Standards statements, key language uses, language expectations, and proficiency level descriptors.

Standards statements describe the language used within the school setting for learning. The key language uses, including *narrate*, *inform*, *argue*, and *explain*, reflect the most prominent ways language is used across different disciplinary areas. The key language uses of *explain* and *argue* are the most relevant in the STEAM context. Language expectations, broken down into the interpretive and expressive modes of communication, provide specific goals to make language learning in the disciplinary areas visible.

The six proficiency level descriptors outline a continuum of language progression as students engage in tasks aimed at meeting language expectations. Table 1.3 explains what the language proficiency levels mean and what students can do at each level. Grounded in an asset-based approach, the WIDA Can-Do Descriptors (2016) emphasize what MLs are capable of achieving with their linguistic knowledge and experiences, rather than focusing on their deficits in English. One important consideration is that we need to document the student's language proficiency levels not only in English but also in the other languages they know. Since WIDA primarily focuses on English, we have adapted the WIDA (2016) Can-Do Descriptors in Table 1.3 to demonstrate what MLs can achieve with academic tasks in any language.

Table 1.3 provides general Can-Do Descriptors for MLs, illustrating what MLs can accomplish socially and academically in school contexts by the end of each language proficiency level. Since all of our sample MLs were bilingual or multilingual, it is important to mention that their ability to perform academic tasks may vary significantly between languages. For example, Lin is at the Beginning level in his primary language, Chinese, while at the Emerging level in English in the domains of reading and writing. This indicates that Lin could comprehend more complex texts and express more sophisticated ideas in Chinese than he could in English.

Table 1.3 Language Proficiency Levels and Can-Do Descriptors (Adapted From WIDA, 2016)

Language Proficiency Level	General Can-Do Descriptors
Level 1: Entering	Students can understand and use single words or short, memorized phrases to communicate. They rely heavily on modes such as visuals and gestures for meaning.
Level 2: Emerging	Students can understand and use simple phrases or short sentences. They begin to engage in basic conversations or read simple texts with a high level of support.
Level 3: Developing	Students can participate in more structured conversations and understand more complex language in both oral and written forms. They can elaborate ideas with more details with consistent support.
Level 4: Expanding	Students can demonstrate increasing independence in using the oral and written language. They can engage in academic conversations and comprehend grade-level content with some support.
Level 5: Bridging	Students can use oral and written language effectively for a wide range of academic and social purposes with minimal support. They can engage in academic tasks such as discussions, analyze texts, and produce clear and coherent writing.
Level 6: Reaching	Students can show the level of language proficiency comparable to native speakers in academic settings. They can communicate and understand complex academic language in all subject areas without the need for support.

We will elaborate in the remainder of this book on how to use the WIDA resources and the ELD standards on grade-level clusters at the elementary level.

NGSS, NCAS, and WIDA Connections

The primary focus of STEAM learning is typically placed on understanding and applying concepts related to these disciplines rather than prioritizing the acquisition of language skills. The main objective is to develop a deep understanding of scientific principles and technological applications, engineering principles, and mathematical concepts. While language is undoubtedly involved in the communication of STEAM ideas and concepts, it is often considered a means to convey knowledge rather than the central focus of the learning process. NCAS complements NGSS and WIDA standards by fostering interdisciplinary learning that connects linguistic and scientific competencies with artistic expression. For example, when students design environmentally sustainable solutions as part of an NGSS-aligned project, they can leverage NCAS-aligned activities such as creating visual representations, composing explanatory narratives, or using digital tools to convey their ideas creatively. This alignment ensures that MLs not only access the content but also develop critical 21st-century skills like collaboration, communication, and cultural awareness, enriching their STEAM education experience.

In STEM fields, the emphasis tends to be on the development of analytical and problem-solving skills, critical thinking, and hands-on experimentation, with language serving as a tool for expressing and communicating complex ideas rather than as a primary learning outcome. NGSS and WIDA ELD standards are closely related in their emphasis on integrating content and language instruction (see Table 1.4), supporting language development across academic disciplines, and promoting access to high-quality education for all students, including MLs. By aligning these standards and implementing integrated instructional approaches, teachers can create inclusive learning environments where language support is embedded and all students have equitable access to high-quality science education.

Furthermore, this approach emphasizes the significance of communication in STEAM endeavors, highlighting that students are expected to interact with their peers in a specific manner to facilitate the development of explanations and the use of models. To illustrate, when students analyze weather patterns to formulate a renewable energy solution, their involvement goes beyond mere analysis of data. They are required to construct a model to articulate their thought process and experiment with their concepts. This process not only allows students to enhance their scientific knowledge but also enables them to grasp content-specific scientific languages. The interconnectedness of language skills, science and engineering practices, and communication requirements in the STEAM project is evident.

Table 1.4 Examples of NGSS, NCAS, and WIDA Connection

Language Domains	NGSS Science and Engineering Practices	NCAS	WIDA Language Expectation
Interpretive	SEP 7: Engaging in Argument From Evidence • Compare and refine arguments based on an evaluation of the evidence presented. • Distinguish among facts, reasoned judgment based on research findings, and speculation in an explanation.	Responding • Perceive and analyze artistic work. • Interpret intent and meaning in artistic work. • Apply criteria to evaluate artistic work. Connecting • Synthesize and relate knowledge and personal experiences to make art. • Relate artistic ideas and works with societal, cultural, and historical context to deepen understanding.	ELD-SC 4-5 Argue.Interpretive Interpret scientific arguments by • Identifying relevant evidence from data, models, and/or information from investigations of phenomena or design solutions. • Comparing reasoning and claims based on evidence. • Distinguishing among facts, reasoned judgment based on research findings, and speculation in an explanation.
Expressive	SEP 7: Engaging in Argument From Evidence • Construct and/or support an argument with evidence, data, and/or a model. • Use data to evaluate claims about cause and effect. • Make a claim about the merit of a solution to a problem by citing relevant evidence about how it meets the criteria and constraints of the problem.	Creating • Generate and conceptualize artistic ideas and work. • Organize and develop artistic ideas and work. • Refine and complete artistic work. Performing/Presenting/Producing • Select, analyze, and interpret artistic work for presentation. • Develop and refine artistic techniques and work for presentation. • Convey meaning through the presentation of artistic work.	ELD-SC 4-5 Argue.Expressive Construct scientific arguments that • Introduce topic/phenomenon in issues related to the natural and designed world(s). • Make and define a claim based on evidence, data, and/or model. • Establish a neutral tone or an objective stance. • Signal logical relationships among reasoning, relevant evidence, data, and/or a model when making between claim, evidence, and reasoning.

Conclusion

Integrating STEAM education into the elementary curriculum offers valuable opportunities to support MLs' content and language development. By embracing MLs' diverse cultures and languages and providing meaningful learning experiences, STEAM teachers can create inclusive and equitable learning environments where all students thrive. The alignment of NGSS, NCAS, and WIDA standards provides a solid foundation for designing STEAM instruction that meets the diverse needs of MLs, fostering their engagement, confidence, and success in STEAM disciplines and beyond. As teachers continue to explore innovative approaches to STEAM education, it is essential to prioritize the linguistic and cultural diversity of students, recognizing it as a strength and asset in the learning process.

References

Allina, B. (2017). The development of STEAM educational policy to promote student creativity and social empowerment. *Arts Education Policy Review, 119*, 77–87. https://doi.org/10.1080/10632913.2017.1296392

Avgerinou, M. D. (2001). Towards a visual literacy index. In R. E. Griffin, V. S. Williams & L. Jung (Eds.), *Exploring the visual future: Art design, science & technology* (pp. 17–26). IVLA.

Avgerinou, M. D., & Pettersson, R. (2011). Toward a cohesive theory of visual literacy. *Journal of Visual Literacy, 30*(2), 1–19.

Bialik, K., & Scheller, A., & Walker, K. (2018). *6 facts about English language learners in U.S. public schools*. Pew Research. https://www.pewresearch.org/short-reads/2018/10/25/6-facts-about-english-language-learners-in-u-s-public-schools/

Chen, C. S., & Lin, J. W. (2019). A practical action research study of the impact of maker-centered STEM-PjBL on a rural middle school in Taiwan. *International Journal of Science and Mathematics Education, 17*(1), 85–108.

Chen, X. N., & Newman, M. (2022). *Teaching social studies to multilingual learners in middle school: Connecting inquiry and visual literacy to promote progressive learning*. Rowman & Littlefield.

English, L. D. (2016). STEM education K-12: Perspectives on integration. *International Journal of STEM Education, 3*, 1–8.

Erduran, S. (2020). Nature of "STEM"? Epistemic underpinnings of integrated science, technology, engineering, and mathematics in education. *Science & Education, 29*, 781–784.

Fillmore, L. W. (2000). Loss of family languages: Should educators be concerned? *Theory Into Practice, 39*, 203–210. DOI:10.2307/1477339

Grapin, S. E., Llosa, L., Haas, A., Goggins, M., & Lee, O. (2019). Precision: Toward a meaning-centered view of language use with English learners in the content areas. *Linguistics and Education, 50*, 71–83.

Hacıoğlu, Y., & Gülhan, F. (2021). The effects of STEM education on the students' critical thinking skills and STEM perceptions. *Journal of Education in Science Environment and Health, 7*(2), 139–155.

Hall, E. T. (1976). *Beyond culture.* Anchor.

Halliday, M. A. K. (1975). *Learning how to mean: Explorations in the development of language.* Edward Arnold. http://dx.doi.org/10.1016/b978-0-12-443701-2.50025-1

Halliday, M. A. K., & Hasan, R. (1985). *Language, context, and text: Aspects of language in a social-semiotic perspective.* Deakin University Press.

Heath, S. B. (1983). *Ways with words: Language, life, and work in communities and classrooms.* Cambridge University Press.

Herro, D., Quigley, C., & Cian, H. (2018). The challenges of STEAM instruction: Lessons from the field. *Action in Teacher Education, 41*, 172–190. https://doi.org/10.1080/01626620.2018.1551159

Jackson, C., Mohr-Schroeder, M. J., Bush, S. B., Maiorca, C., Roberts, T., Yost, C., & Fowler, A. (2021). Equity-oriented conceptual framework for K-12 STEM literacy. *International Journal of STEM Education, 8*, 1–16.

Korhonen, V. (2023). *Percentage of children who speak another language than English at home in the U.S. in 2019, by poverty status.* https://www.statista.com/statistics/476863/children-who-speak-another-language-than-english-at-home-in-the-us-by-poverty-status/#statisticContainer

Lee, O., & Stephens, A. (2020). English learners in STEM subjects: Contemporary views on STEM subjects and language with English learners. *Educational Researcher, 49*(6), 426–432. DOI:10.3102/0013189X20923708

Li, Y., Wang, K., Xiao, Y., & Froyd, J. E. (2020). Research and trends in STEM education: A systematic review of journal publications. *International Journal of STEM Education, 7*(1), 1–16.

National Academies of Sciences, Engineering, and Medicine (NASEM). (2018). *English learners in STEM subjects: Transforming classrooms, schools, and lives.* National Academies Press.

National Center for Educational Statistics (NCES). (2023). *English learners in public schools.* https://nces.ed.gov/programs/coe/indicator/cgf/english-learners

National Center for Science and Engineering Statistics (NCSES). (2023). *Diversity and STEM: Women, minorities, and persons with disabilities 2023* [Special report]. National Science Foundation, NSF 23-315. https://ncses.nsf.gov/pubs/nsf23315/

National Coalition for Core Arts Standards (NCAS). (2014). *National Core Arts Standards: A conceptual framework for arts learning.* National Art Education Association.

National Governors Association Center for Best Practices & Council of Chief State School Officers. (2010). *Common Core State Standards: Mathematics.* https://www.corestandards.org/math/

NGSS Lead States. (2013). *Next Generation Science Standards: For states, by states.* National Academies Press.

Quigley, C., & Herro, D. (2016). "Finding the joy in the unknown": Implementation of STEAM teaching practices in middle school science and math classrooms. *Journal of Science Education and Technology, 25,* 410–426. https://doi.org/10.1007/S10956-016-9602-Z

Quintero, D., & Hansen, M. (2021). *As we tackle school segregation, don't forget about English language learners.* Brown Center Chalkboard. https://www.brookings.edu/articles/as-we-tackle-school-segregation-dont-forget-about-english-learner-students/

Reiser, B. J. (2012). *A framework for K-12 science education: Practices, crosscutting concepts, and core ideas.* National Research Council, Board on Science Education, Division of Behavioral and Social Sciences and Education.

Roehrig, G. H., Dare, E. A., & Ring-Whalen, E. (2021). Understanding coherence and integration in integrated STEM curriculum. *International Journal of STEM Education, 8*(1), Article 2.

Simoncini, K., & Lasen, M. (2018). Ideas about STEM among Australian early childhood professionals: How important is STEM in early childhood education? *International Journal of Early Childhood, 50*(3), 353–369.

Takeuchi, M. A., Sengupta, P., Shanahan, M. C., Adams, J. D., & Hachem, M. (2020). Transdisciplinarity in STEM education: A critical review. *Studies in Science Education, 56*(2), 213–253.

Tytler, R. (2020). STEM education for the twenty-first century. In J. Anderson & Y. Li (Eds.), *Integrated Approaches to STEM Education: An International Perspective* (pp. 21–43). Springer.

US Department of Education. (2016). *Newcomer tool kit.* https://www2. ed.gov/about/offices/list/oela/newcomers-toolkit/ncomertoolkit.pdf

Vygotsky, L. S. (1978). The prehistory of written language. In M. Cole, V. John-Steiner, S. Scribner & E. Souberman (Eds.), *Mind in society: The development of higher psychological processes* (pp. 103–119). Harvard University Press.

WIDA. (2016). *Can do descriptors: Key uses edition.* https://wida.wisc.edu/ sites/default/files/resource/CanDo-KeyUses-Gr-2-3.pdf

WIDA. (2020). *English Language Development (ELD) Standards Framework, 2020 edition: Kindergarten-grade 12.* Board of the University of Wisconsin System. https://wida.wisc.edu/teach/standards/eld

WIDA. (2024). *WIDA mission and history.* https://wida.wisc.edu/about/ mission-history

2

The ESEM Framework for MLs' STEAM Learning

In this chapter, we use Mr. Gilbert and Ms. Fang's classroom vignette as an example while exploring what the Equitable STEAM Education for Multilingual Learners (ESEM) Framework is and how it can be applied. The school context, teachers' backgrounds, and selected ML profiles are presented in Table 2.1.

Table 2.1 Class Profile 2

Context	Suburban, 3rd grade, ESL pull-out and push-in model
Teachers	**Mr. Gilbert** (a monolingual English speaker) **and Ms. Fang** (a bilingual ESL teacher)

Selected ML Profiles	**Olha**
	• Born in Ukraine but moved with her family to the US six months ago. Olha is considered a newcomer.
	• **Ukrainian**
	  ◦ Oracy: expanding
	  ◦ Literacy: developing
	• **English**
	  ◦ Oracy: emerging
	  ◦ Literacy: entering
	
	Lin
	• Born in Australia to Chinese parents and moved back to China when he was five years old. The family immigrated to the US one year ago.
	• **Chinese**
	  ◦ Oracy: developing
	  ◦ Literacy: beginning
	• **English**
	  ◦ Oracy: developing
	  ◦ Literacy: emerging

Mr. Gilbert embarked on an effort to integrate STEAM into the ELA curriculum. To do so, he selected the appropriate NGSS standards before designing the unit using an inquiry model (e.g., the 5E learning cycle, Bybee, 2013). The unit started by immersing the students in children's books, delving into the topic of severe weather. Following this, Mr. Gilbert curated a variety of rain gear that enable people to cope with wet weather conditions. Subsequently, he presented a challenge to all students to design innovative rain gear. As the ESL push-in teacher, Ms. Fang supported the MLs, including Olha and Lin. The support was focused on explaining key concepts through multimedia or students' primary languages, practicing the use of academic vocabulary, and engaging in disciplinary discourses through sentence stems.

The above vignette provides a glimpse of how an integrated STEAM unit was implemented in a diverse elementary classroom. However, we wonder whether the unit was designed and delivered through an equity and social justice lens. Further, were MLs positively positioned and fully supported to engage in the learning process? To enhance the inclusivity and effectiveness of the unit, this chapter introduces a practical teaching framework and illustrates its implementation in this third-grade classroom. The companion website provides additional resources related to the topics in this chapter. We will first delve into the theoretical and pedagogical approaches that underpin the ESEM Framework.

What Are the Relevant Theoretical and Pedagogical Approaches?

Culturally and Linguistically Responsive Teaching (CLRT)

Culturally and linguistically responsive teaching (CLRT) is an integrated theoretical perspective essential for fostering equity in teaching and learning. CLRT synthesizes key ideas from culturally responsive teaching (CRT) (Gay, 2002) and linguistically responsive teaching (LRT) (Lucas & Villegas, 2010). We will describe each of the perspectives and explain the need to adopt the combined stance with research evidence.

There are several equity-related issues concerning diversity in STEAM. On the one hand, MLs tend to have lower interest in STEM, lower persistence rates to pursue STEM at the higher education level, and a lower sense of belonging in STEM classes (Dost, 2024; NASEM, 2018). On the other hand, there is a strong need to enhance the diversity of both curriculum content and professionals within the STEAM education field (Margolis et al., 2010; Vakil, 2018) and address gender and race disparity (National Center for Educational Statistics, 2023). Many potential factors contribute to this area of need, including (1) inadequate teacher preparation and professional development for STEAM educators (Buxton & Lee, 2014; Goodson et al., 2019; NASEM, 2020); (2) inequitable access (English, 2017; Jackson et al., 2021; Ramsay-Jordan, 2020); and (3) cultural relevance (Moldavan & Gupta, 2024; Vielma, 2023).

First, elementary educators are predominantly prepared as generalists and frequently enroll in teacher education programs with limited confidence and interest in instructing STEAM subjects (Poland et al., 2017; Zimmerman, 2016). As a result, they often rely on interactive, hands-on activities to ensure effective STEAM teaching in their classrooms. However, the inconsistency of this approach may result in student confusion and a fragmented learning journey. Recognizing the issue, it becomes imperative to provide professional preparation and development using a unified framework for STEAM instruction. The framework that we propose in this book plays an important role in ensuring a coherent and structured educational experience for students across diverse situations, bridging any potential gaps arising from the diverse backgrounds and training of teachers.

Second, access to quality STEAM education is not evenly distributed, particularly across different communities and socioeconomic backgrounds (Jho et al., 2016). Students from underprivileged areas might lack the resources, facilities, and qualified teachers required for inclusive STEAM instruction. This inequality in access perpetuates educational disparities and limits for students who could otherwise excel in STEAM fields. The issue of inequity also stems from both race and gender. Rainey et al. (2018) found that women and students from racial and ethnic minority backgrounds experience significant underrepresentation and historical exclusion within STEM fields. This lack of representation can be attributed to a multitude of factors, such as cultural norms, organizational structures, and unequal access to quality education (Casad et al., 2020; Prain & Waldrip, 2006).

Third, there are limited STEAM curricula that take into account the cultural backgrounds, experiences, and interests of the diverse student population. A curriculum that does not resonate with students' lives can lead to disengagement and decreased motivation to pursue STEAM subjects (Lin & Tsai, 2020). STEAM curricula should center on the goal of promoting equity and social justice (Davis & Haverly, 2022; NASEM, 2022). To achieve this goal, we need qualified and proficient teachers who are trained in CRT to develop the justice-focused curricula (NASEM, 2020, 2022), facilitate student learning, and inspire historically underrepresented minorities to pursue STEM majors and careers (Reider et al., 2021; Shillingford et al., 2017).

CRT is developed based on the assumption that "when academic knowledge and skills are situated within the lived experiences and frames of reference of students, they are more personally meaningful, have higher interest appeal, and are learned more easily and thoroughly" (Gay, 2002, p. 106). Aligned with the concept of funds of knowledge (González et al., 2005) as an asset-based, equity-centered approach, CRT focuses on acknowledging and leveraging "the cultural characteristics, experiences, and perspectives of ethnically diverse students as conduits for teaching them more effectively" (Gay, 2002, p. 106).

CRT is a broad pedagogical approach that extends beyond classroom instruction and assessment practices. It emphasizes building a welcoming learning community, adapting cross-cultural communication styles, fostering inclusivity, and recognizing the importance of cultural awareness in all aspects of teaching and learning (Gay, 2002; Lee et al., 2008). A primary goal of CRT is to achieve equitable educational outcomes and promote social justice for all (Hernandez et al., 2013; Ladson-Billings, 1995).

CRT is critical for enhancing MLs' learning outcomes, as supported by research evidence in the STEM field. For example, Torres-Velasquez and Lobo (2005) investigated the efficacy of implementing culturally responsive mathematics teaching for ELLs. Their findings revealed that integrating mathematics with students' life experiences and employing mathematical tools to foster a learning community were highly effective in culturally diverse classrooms. The key to implementing CRT is to purposefully establish connections with students' cultural knowledge and utilize these funds of knowledge to enrich their school learning (Lee & Buxton, 2010; Roe, 2019).

While CRT strongly emphasizes building on students' cultural knowledge and lived experiences to enhance disciplinary learning, MLs concurrently grapple with the challenge of developing proficiency in more than one language. This is why we need to consider linguistically responsive teaching (LRT) as a pedagogical approach where teachers recognize and address the language demands on MLs (Lucas & Villegas, 2010) to ensure equity and linguistic justice in teaching and learning. It is important to develop educators' essential orientations, knowledge, and skills, such as (1) understanding the diverse language backgrounds and proficiency levels present in classrooms; (2) creating an inclusive learning environment where diverse linguistic skills are recognized and valued; and (3) providing explicit and differentiated instruction to support MLs' multilingualism and multiliteracy development (Lucas & Villegas, 2010). When teachers regard both cultural and linguistic diversity as valuable assets contributing to academic success, they can purposefully plan and provide support to enhance MLs' content learning and language development (Echevarria et al., 2006).

A related concept to linguistic justice is translanguaging. Traditionally, MLs' proficiency in multiple languages was assumed to be kept in separate entities with rigid boundaries (Poza, 2016). This view is reflected in the design and implementation of many bilingual programs where students use English only during the "English" block and switch to Spanish only during the "Spanish" block. With new research on the nature of language development and MLs' language practices, translanguaging emerges as a robust theoretical and pedagogical approach that challenges the traditional view. It is defined as "the multiple discursive practices that bilinguals use to make sense of their bilingual worlds" (García, 2009, p. 45). In practice, MLs tap into their full linguistic and other semiotic resources (e.g., visuals, gestures, facial expressions, and sound) to communicate meaning. The choice of named languages (e.g., Spanish and English) and modality is based on who the audience is, what the purpose is, and how to effectively convey the information.

Drawing data from the interactions among fifth graders in a bilingual Spanish and English science classroom, Poza (2016) documented that the bilingual students' language uses are dynamic and flexible in that they frequently disregard prescribed language boundaries and draw from all linguistic repertoire to enhance content knowledge and academic skills, including various discursive styles. Poza's (2016) findings showed that "translanguaging practices support students in their development of scientific content knowledge and skills" (p. 3). Further, Poza (2016) made a cautionary note that to bring translanguaging to the central stage, it is critical to offer authentic experiences, extensive collaboration, and exposure to various target language varieties.

Translanguaging is a justice-focused approach. It not only validates MLs' diverse linguistic resources and promotes multilingualism but also provides opportunities for all students to develop metalinguistic skills, which refer to the abilities to analyze and reflect on how different languages work and how to best improve their own language learning (García et al., 2016). Further, with proper professional development, it is possible for teachers to create a translanguaging classroom even if they are not proficient in MLs' primary languages (see examples in García et al., 2016, and in Part II of this book).

Having explained CRT, LRT, and translanguaging, we advocate for the integration of these perspectives into one teaching framework, with support from research in different disciplinary areas. Lee et al. (2008) developed an instructional congruence framework for science learning, incorporating elements from CRT and LRT. This framework underscores the significance of providing MLs access to their primary languages and cultures, emphasizing the use of comprehensible input, engaging instructional materials, and research-based strategies. Driver and Powell's (2017) study explored a word-problem intervention rooted in CLRT for ELLs facing challenges in mathematics, resulting in significant improvements in their ability to solve word problems. Guided by CLRT principles, Sanford et al. (2020) designed multitiered support systems for English learners in mathematics, leading to substantial advancements in accurately identifying vocabulary words and solving story problems among participating students.

5E Learning Cycle in STEAM Education

The 5E learning cycle (Bybee, 2013; Bybee et al., 2006) is an instructional model designed to engage students in the learning process through a series of stages: engage, explore, explain, elaborate, and evaluate. The 5E model is often associated with inquiry-based learning and widely used in science education, but it can be adapted for other disciplines as well. Here is a brief overview of each stage.

1. Engage: The learning begins with a question or a phenomenon that captures students' attention and stimulates their prior knowledge. This phase is intended to pique curiosity and make connections between existing knowledge and the upcoming topic.
2. Explore: Students are encouraged to explore concepts and materials through hands-on activities, experiments, or investigations. This phase is characterized by active learning, allowing students to make observations, collect data, and ask questions.
3. Explain: Following exploration, students discuss their findings and observations. Teachers introduce formal concepts, explanations, and relevant vocabulary to help students build a solid understanding of the topic.
4. Elaborate: Students deepen their understanding by applying the newly acquired knowledge in different contexts or extending their learning through additional activities. This phase often involves more complex tasks and challenges that require critical thinking and problem-solving skills.
5. Evaluate: The final stage involves assessing students' understanding of the topic. The assessment can take various forms, such as quizzes, projects, presentations, or discussions. Evaluation helps both students and teachers gauge the effectiveness of the teaching and learning experience.

In the context of STEAM education, the 5E learning cycle is considered critical (Eroglu & Bektas, 2022; Schallert et al., 2021) for several reasons, including its effectiveness in visualizing thinking processes. First, the model actively promotes inquiry-based learning, aligning seamlessly with the principles of encouraging students to ask questions, explore, and independently discover knowledge. It immerses students in disciplinary practices and supports students' development of their identities as STEM professionals (NASEM, 2018). Second, the emphasis on hands-on and active learning experiences serves as a powerful tool for visualizing abstract concepts in STEAM, allowing students to see and interact with theoretical ideas, thereby enhancing comprehension. Third, by integrating components from science, technology, engineering, arts, and mathematics, the 5E model not only fosters an interconnected perspective but also enables students to visualize the convergence of these disciplines in real-world applications. Moreover, the model accommodates diverse learning styles, providing a platform for visual thinkers to thrive through various activities and stages. The incorporation of visual aspects in the 5E learning cycle enhances students' ability to conceptualize complex ideas and reinforces the development of critical thinking skills. In essence, the 5E learning cycle emerges as a comprehensive and dynamic approach, where visualizing thinking processes plays a crucial role in unlocking the full potential of STEAM education.

From an equity and social justice lens, the 5E learning cycle can provide actionable approaches (Davis & Haverly, 2022) to encourage collaborative inquiry and foster a supportive learning environment where all students feel included and valued. By fostering collaboration and peer interaction, students with diverse backgrounds feel empowered to engage with science and contribute their unique perspectives.

Beginning with engagement, teachers share puzzling phenomena to increase identity and representation in science by providing opportunities for students to explore science concepts and fostering a sense of belonging. Through exploration, students are encouraged to investigate concepts independently while receiving guidance to critically evaluate their thoughts and consider alternative viewpoints. In the explanation phase, students are prompted to justify their ideas using collected evidence, fostering deeper understanding and critical thinking skills. In the elaboration and evaluation stages, students are asked to connect their learning to real-world applications, recognizing science's essential role in promoting social justice and enabling them to contribute meaningfully to equitable solutions beyond the classroom.

Overall, the 5E learning cycle serves as a powerful approach for promoting equity and social justice in STEAM education, from increasing opportunities and access to enhancing identity and representation, expanding the boundaries of scientific inquiry, and fostering a vision of science as a tool for justice and empowerment.

Critical Visual Literacy

We briefly introduced the concept of visual literacy in Chapter 1. Visual literacy is closely connected to the STEM field (Riddle, 2021), as students are often expected to view and analyze a data chart or create a sketch of a model. Visual literacy involves a set of skills that people need in order to work with visuals. The basic visual literacy skills can be generally broken down into three categories: "reading" *with* visuals, "writing" in visual formats, and visual thinking. The left column of Table 2.2 elaborates on what each of these categories entails.

In contrast, critical visual literacy moves beyond the basic visual literacy skills and integrates a critical component (see the right column of Table 2.2). Chung (2013) explains that critical visual literacy invites viewers to delve into political, social, economic, and cultural dimensions and evaluate how and why the visual representation reflects power dynamics within the context. When students read visuals, they read *against* visuals (Newfield, 2011) to not only identify what the message is but also consider the social, cultural, and political contexts to evaluate the power relations. For example, while viewing green space in local communities on the justice map (https://www.justicemap.org/), students analyze the impact of factors such as race and income on environmental challenges.

Furthermore, an important goal for critical visual literacy is to challenge the status quo and promote social changes (Chung, 2013; Kim & Serrano, 2017; Santos Costa & Xavier, 2016). When students write in a visual format, they actively engage in challenging the existing power relations and creating counternarratives to promote social justice. All of

Table 2.2 Visual Literacy vs. Critical Visual Literacy

Visual Literacy	Critical Visual Literacy
"Reading" with the visuals to make sense, analyze, synthesize, and evaluate information	"Reading" against the visuals to analyze, question, and reflect on the power relations in visual representations, considering the social, cultural, and political contexts
"Writing" visuals to communicate learning in visual formats	"Writing" visuals to create counternarratives to advocate for and promote social justice
Visual thinking: The thinking process involving how to effectively "read" visuals to gather information and "write" ideas visually to communicate learning	Critical visual thinking: The thinking process emphasizing how to synthesize, question, and evaluate power relations based on contextual factors and re-create visual narratives that challenge the status quo

the high-level analytical thinking involved in "reading against" visuals and "writing" visually falls under critical visual thinking.

With regard to STEAM education, critical visual literacy not only equips MLs with essential academic skills and access to the core curriculum but also empowers them to act as advocates for equity and social justice. To scaffold critical visual literacy development, our recommendation is to take a sequential approach. It is not always possible to go through the entire set of critical visual skills while working with one visual or in one lesson. Neither is it necessary. However, it is crucial to provide opportunities for students to interact with a variety of visuals in the curriculum, emphasize the contextual factors associated with the messages, and integrate a social action component.

In summary, we have outlined fundamental concepts, components, and associated research regarding the impact of CLRT, including translanguaging, the 5E learning cycle, and critical visual literacy, on the STEAM learning experiences of MLs. The common thread among these approaches is their learner-centered, inquiry-based, and asset-oriented focus, which aims to advance equity and social justice for all students. These approaches lay the groundwork for us to develop the practical framework in the next section.

What Is the Equitable STEAM Education for Multilingual Learners Framework?

Informed by the theoretical and pedagogical approaches discussed above, the Equitable STEAM Education for Multilingual Learners (ESEM) Framework is designed to empower teachers to effectively and equitably support and engage MLs in STEAM (see Figure 2.1).

The components of the ESEM Framework are presented in Figure 2.1 and will be explained below.

- The ESEM Framework has several interconnected components. Inside the box of Figure 2.1 are four circles representing the core principles informed by the integrated approaches of CLRT, 5E, and critical visual literacy presented in the previous section. They are:

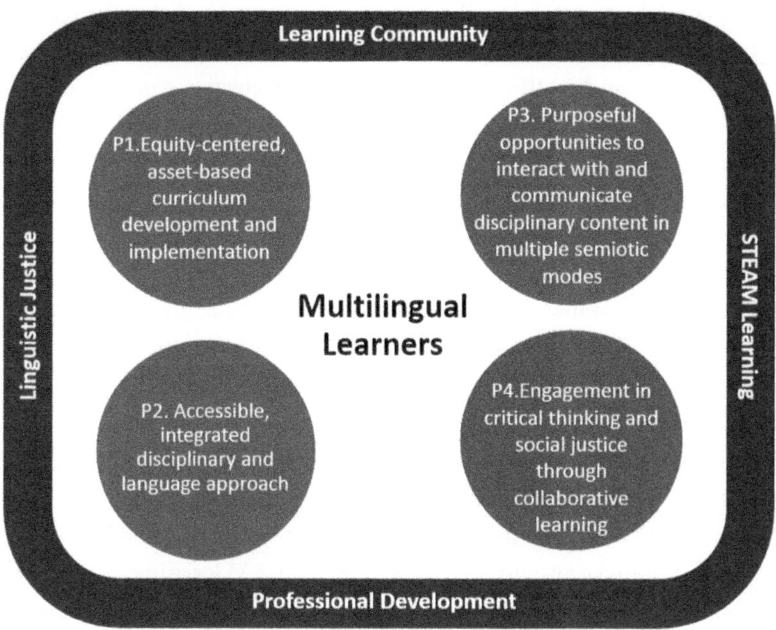

Figure 2.1 The Equitable STEAM Education for Multilingual Learners (ESEM) Framework

- Principle 1. Equity-centered, asset-based curriculum development and implementation
- Principle 2. Accessible, integrated disciplinary and language approach
- Principle 3. Purposeful opportunities to interact with and communicate disciplinary content in multiple semiotic modes
- Principle 4. Engagement in critical thinking and social justice through collaborative learning

These four core principles jointly guide teachers toward the goal of fostering equity and social justice in STEAM teaching and learning for MLs.

The four sides of the ESEM framework are delineated with different components, each providing sociocultural, linguistic, disciplinary, and professional contexts, respectively, for the core principles. Positioned at the top is "learning community." This has two layers of meaning. The first layer is the school community, which refers to the network of professionals and individuals associated with a particular school. These partners share a common interest in supporting the education and well-being of students.

The second layer refers to the broader community that may have an impact on the school. This includes a wider range of residents, businesses, organizations, and institutions. Together, these entities contribute to the fabric of the community and play a role in supporting and expanding students' funds of knowledge (Moll et al., 1992). This component will be explored more in Chapter 3.

"Professional development" is positioned at the bottom. This refers to the continuous programs, activities, and opportunities to enhance the knowledge, skills, and effectiveness of education professionals. This component will be further discussed in Chapter 8. On the left-hand side is "linguistic justice," a term advocated by Baker-Bell (2020) as an alternative to "language support" to better align with broader social justice objectives by integrating MLs' linguistic resources and needs into teaching and learning. "STEAM learning" is positioned on the right-hand side of the box, representing the disciplinary context of the framework. The components of "linguistic justice" and "STEAM learning" will be fully integrated into each of the chapters in this book.

To support teachers in implementing the framework in STEAM teaching and learning for MLs, we further identify key teaching practices associated with each of the core principles. These key teaching practices is presented in Table 2.3.

How Do Teachers Apply the ESEM Framework?

We have presented the ESEM Framework and explained the meaning and relationship among its various components. Below we will revisit the opening vignette and demonstrate what teaching and learning look like before and after implementing the core principles and relevant teaching practices from the framework. Table 2.4 shows the comparison between before and after.

By showcasing examples from this third-grade classroom and demonstrating how the implementation of the ESEM Framework can transform MLs' STEAM learning experience, we illustrate how teachers can design teaching and learning centered on equity, fully leveraging and bringing justice to MLs' rich cultural and linguistic assets. Moreover, we demonstrate how educators can empower MLs by activating their agency, encouraging them to develop actions that contribute to the well-being of both local and global communities.

Table 2.3 Key Teaching Practices Supporting Each Core Principle

Core Principles	P1. Equity-centered, asset-based curriculum development and implementation	P3. Purposeful opportunities to interact with and communicate disciplinary content in multiple semiotic modes
Key Teaching Practices	1. Ensure that curriculum content is relevant, inclusive, and accessible to all students. 2. Design learning units that are informed by standards and critical issues in the local and global communities. 3. Develop learning experiences that reflect and build on the cultural and linguistic assets of MLs and diverse disciplinary practices. 4. Provide opportunities for MLs to see themselves reflected positively in the curriculum and learning environment. 5. Implement teaching strategies that recognize and value MLs' linguistic and cultural assets.	1. Design interactive learning experiences that immerse MLs in a diverse range of semiotic modes. 2. Provide differentiated multimodal disciplinary content adaptive to MLs' learning preferences and linguistic needs. 3. Integrate technology tools and sense-making resources that support MLs' engagement with disciplinary content. 4. Scaffold MLs' use of multiple semiotic modes to express their understanding of disciplinary concepts and communicate their ideas effectively. 5. Encourage MLs to create and share multimodal projects that demonstrate their understanding of disciplinary concepts and skills and enhanced proficiency in multiple languages.

(Continued)

Table 2.3 (*Continued*)

Core Principles	P2. Accessible, integrated disciplinary and language approach	P4. Engagement in critical thinking and social justice through collaborative learning
Key Teaching Practices	1. Provide explicit instruction on how languages and culture work for disciplines. 2. Scaffold language use in disciplinary contexts, supporting MLs' comprehension and expression throughout investigations. 3. Facilitate repeated exposure to and practice of language within meaningful disciplinary contexts. 4. Provide opportunities for MLs to engage in disciplinary practices (such as scientific inquiry and mathematical problem-solving) by using their languages in different domains. 5. Promote translanguaging as a valid language practice that supports MLs' learning across disciplines.	1. Foster a classroom culture that respects each other, values critical thinking, and builds community. 2. Encourage MLs to critically examine issues of power, privilege, and inequality in a disciplinary context. 3. Facilitate collaborative learning experiences that promote critical inquiry, evaluate multiple perspectives, and build empathy. 4. Provide opportunities for MLs to generate evidence-based arguments on social justice topics, drawing on their diverse cultural perspectives and experiences. 5. Encourage MLs to take action on social justice issues that have impact on their communities, promoting agency and advocacy.

Table 2.4 Before and After Implementation of the ESEM Framework

Applied Teaching Practices	Before	After
P1: Equity-centered, asset-based curriculum development and implementation		
P1.2 Design learning units that are informed by standards and critical issues in the local and global communities.	Mr. Gilbert started the planning of the unit by selecting the relevant NGSS standards. Ms. Fang supported MLs' English language development based on the ELD standards in WIDA. The link between the unit topic and the critical issue in the community was not explicitly identified.	Mr. Gilbert and Ms. Fang co-planned the unit using both the NGSS and WIDA standards. They co-created integrated learning objectives that enabled students to use languages to engage in disciplinary practices. The unit topic was decided because of the weather challenge faced by the local community.
P1.3 Develop learning experiences that reflect and build on the cultural and linguistic assets of MLs and diverse disciplinary practices.	Mr. Gilbert considered students' prior knowledge, age, and interests while selecting the topic and designing the unit. MLs were viewed as students who needed additional help to develop proficiency in English.	Mr. Gilbert and Ms. Fang designed the unit in a way that acknowledged and valued diversity. They considered factors such as the MLs' cultural and linguistic assets and included how different cultures used local resources to develop rain gear to cope with wet weather condition (e.g., the Chinese conical hat, the Dutch clog, and the Japanese geta). MLs were positioned as valuable members of the learning community. For instance, Lin, who was born in Australia but moved to China, was encouraged to share his firsthand experiences and insights on one of the cultural artifacts, the Chinese conical hat.
P1.5 Implement teaching strategies that recognize and value MLs' linguistic and cultural assets.	Mr. Gilbert did not actively integrate MLs' cultural knowledge and lived experiences into teaching and learning.	Mr. Gilbert and Ms. Fang actively integrated MLs' cultural knowledge and lived experiences into their teaching. The lesson engaged students by highlighting how people from different cultures contribute to the advancement of the STEAM field. When they designed new rain gear as a solution to the wet weather challenge, the students were encouraged to explore their own cultural resources and leverage them to develop their inventions.

(Continued)

Table 2.4 (*Continued*)

Applied Teaching Practices	Before	After
P2: Accessible, integrated disciplinary and language approach		
P2.2 Scaffold language use in disciplinary contexts, supporting MLs' comprehension and expression throughout investigations.	Students were grouped based on their reading levels. MLs were grouped together so Ms. Fang could provide language support.	When assigning students to work on collaborative projects, students who shared the primary language were grouped together to enhance the precision of STEAM discourses, which sometimes may be hindered by MLs' emerging proficiency in English. In Olha and Lin's cases, both of them would benefit from the strategy as they had higher language and literacy proficiency in their primary language developed through their continuous education prior to their move to the United States.
P2.4 Provide opportunities for MLs to engage in disciplinary practices (such as scientific inquiry and mathematical problem-solving) by using their languages in different domains.	MLs used English primarily in the receptive domain (i.e., viewing, listening, and reading) while engaging in the disciplinary practices in the 5E learning cycle.	MLs were able to use all languages in both receptive and expressive (i.e., representing, speaking, and writing) domains throughout the 5E learning cycle.
P2.5 Promote translanguaging as a valid language practice that supports MLs' learning across disciplines.	English was the language of instruction. All work should be submitted in English only. Students' primary languages were occasionally used by Ms. Fang as a scaffold for content and English language development.	Mr. Gilbert and Ms. Fang encouraged students to use all the languages and language varieties throughout the learning process. In the exploration and explanation stages, students were able to do research in any language about how the cultural elements were used for the rainwear. In the evaluation stage, students were encouraged to reflect on how and why they used different languages in the lesson.

Table 2.4 (*Continued*)

Applied Teaching Practices	Before	After
P3: Purposeful opportunities to interact with and communicate disciplinary content in multiple semiotic modes		
P3.1 Design interactive learning experiences that immerse MLs in a diverse range of semiotic modes.	Mr. Gilbert selected several types of rain gear featured in children's books to serve as a hook and add variety.	In addition to children's books, Mr. Gilbert and Ms. Fang purposefully selected visuals and artifacts of the traditional rain gear from different cultures to provide multiple means of representation. Some of the visuals integrated meaningful content and language input from students' primary languages. For instance, the teachers purposefully included the cultural artifact of the Chinese conical hat and a visual with Chinese characters as a way to validate Lin's cultural and linguistic assets and empower his positioning as a knowledgeable peer in the classroom.
P3.3 Integrate technology tools and sense-making resources that support MLs' engagement with disciplinary content.	Students used children's books and selected websites to investigate the weather challenge and design a model as a solution.	Students used a variety of resources such as children's books, visuals, cultural artifacts, and interactive videos to make sense of the phenomenon. They used different digital tools to co-construct the rain-gear model, gather feedback from peers and families, and bring the model to life through the 3D printer.
P3.5 Encourage MLs to create and share multimodal projects that demonstrate their understanding of disciplinary concepts and skills and enhanced proficiency in multiple languages.	In the evaluation stage, students designed a 2D rain gear blueprint and presented it to the class.	In the evaluation stage, students designed a 3D rain gear model and shared their design with the school community and families. Students were encouraged to reflect on how their cultural knowledge informed the design of their rain gear. They also reflected on their language choices and effective use of different modes.

(Continued)

Table 2.4 (*Continued*)

Applied Teaching Practices	Before	After
P4: Engagement in critical thinking and social justice through collaborative learning		
P4.2 Encourage MLs to critically examine issues of power, privilege, and inequality in a disciplinary context.	Visuals and other semiotic modes were used primarily as learning aids for content and language development.	Students had access to a set of artifacts and visuals to explore how people from different cultures designed special rain gear to cope with wet weather conditions. The emphasis on contexts propelled students to critically analyze and evaluate their science and engineering designs with consideration of sociocultural factors such as available resources and local weather conditions.
P4.4 Provide opportunities for MLs to generate evidence-based arguments on social justice topics, drawing on their diverse cultural perspectives and experiences.	Students engaged in the claim-evidence-reasoning (CER) discourse pattern throughout the 5E learning cycle, but there was no intentional opportunity for MLs to draw from their own cultural perspectives and experiences.	Students engaged in the CER discourse pattern throughout the 5E learning cycle, and there were multiple opportunities for MLs to draw from their own cultural perspectives and experiences to inform the investigation and innovative design of rain gear.
P4.5 Encourage MLs to take action on social justice issues that have impact on their communities, promoting agency and advocacy.	Students were expected to design an innovative type of rain gear, but it was not connected to a specific community need within a sociocultural context.	Students started the unit with a real-world issue in the community. Through collaboration with and gathering authentic feedback from peers and community members, students revised their design that could serve as the solution to a critical issue faced by the community that was prone to wet weather conditions.

Conclusion

This chapter presents the ESEM Framework informed by the key constructs from CLRT, translanguaging, 5E learning cycle, and critical visual literacy. We describe the components of the ESEM Framework and explain their interconnectedness to highlight their collective impact on promoting MLs' STEAM learning. Moreover, we provide an example of how to implement the framework in a third-grade classroom, showcasing its potential to advance equity and social justice in STEAM education. Part II of this book serves as a practical guide for implementing the ESEM Framework in STEAM education, empowering educators to bring culturally and linguistically inclusive practices to life. Each chapter in that section provides actionable strategies, real-world examples, and templates tailored to diverse educational settings. From curriculum design to professional development, these chapters form a comprehensive roadmap for transforming STEAM education into an equitable and engaging experience for all learners.

References

Baker-Bell, A. (2020). *Linguistic justice: Black language, literacy, identity, and pedagogy*. NCTE-Routledge Research Series. Routledge.

Buxton, C., & Lee, O. (2014). English language learners in science education. In N. Lederman & S. Abell (Eds.), *Handbook of research on science education* (Vol. 2, pp. 204–222). Routledge.

Bybee, R. W. (2013). *Translating the NGSS for classroom instruction*. Corwin.

Bybee, R. W., Taylor, J. A., Gardner, A., Van Scotter, P., Carlson Powell, J., Westbrook, A., & Landes, N. (2006). *BSCS 5E instructional model: Origins and effectiveness*. Office of Science Education, National Institutes of Health.

Casad, B., Franks, J., Garasky, C., Kittleman, M., Roesler, A., Hall, D., & Petzel, Z. (2020). Gender inequality in academia: Problems and solutions for women faculty in STEM. *Journal of Neuroscience Research, 99*, 13–23. https://doi.org/10.1002/jnr.24631

Chung, S. K. (2013). Critical visual literacy. *International Journal of Arts Education, 11*(2), 1–21.

Davis, E. A., & Haverly, C. (2022). Well-started beginners: Preparing elementary teachers for rigorous, consequential, just, and equitable science teaching. In J. Luft & G. Jones (Eds.), *Handbook of research on science teacher education* (pp. 83–96). Routledge.

Dost, G. (2024). Students' perspectives on the "STEM belonging" concept at A-level, undergraduate, and postgraduate levels: An examination of gender and ethnicity in student descriptions. *International Journal of STEM Education, 11*(12). https://doi.org/10.1186/s40594-024-00472-9

Driver, M. K., & Powell, S. R. (2017). Culturally and linguistically responsive schema intervention: Improving word problem solving for English language learners with mathematics difficulty. *Learning Disability Quarterly, 40*(1), 41–53. https://doi.org/10.1177/0731948716646730

Echevarria, J., Short, D., & Powers, K. (2006). School reform and standards-based education: A model for English-language learners. *Journal of Educational Research, 99*(4), 195–211. https://doi.org/10.3200/JOER.99.4.195-211

English, L. (2017). Advancing elementary and middle school STEM education. *International Journal of Science and Mathematics Education, 15*, 5–24. https://doi.org/10.1007/S10763-017-9802-X

Eroglu, S., & Bektas, O. (2022). The effect of 5E-based STEM education on academic achievement, scientific creativity, and views on the nature of science. *Learning and Individual Differences, 98*(7), Article 102181. https://doi.org/10.1016/j.lindif.2022.102181

García, O. (2009). *Bilingual education in the 21st century: A global perspective.* John Wiley & Sons.

García, O., Johnson, S., & Seltzer, K. (2016). *The translanguaging classroom: Leveraging student bilingualism for learning.* Caslon.

Gay, G. (2002). Preparing for culturally-responsive teaching. *Journal of Teacher Education, 53*, 106–116.

González, N., Moll, L., & Amanti, C. (Eds.). (2005). *Funds of knowledge: Theorizing practices in households, communities, and classrooms.* Routledge. https://doi.org/10.4324/9781410613462

Goodson, B., Caswell, L., Price, C., Litwok, D., Dynarski, M., Crowe, E., Meyer, R., & Rice, A. (2019). *Teacher preparation experiences and early teaching effectiveness* (NCEE No. 2019–4007). U.S. Department of Education, Institute of Education Sciences, National Center for Education Evaluation and Regional Assistance. https://eric.ed.gov/?id=ED598664

Hernandez, C. M., Morales, A. R., & Shroyer, M. G. (2013). The development of a model of culturally responsive science and mathematics teaching. *Cultural Studies of Science Education, 8*, 803–820. DOI:10.1007/s11422-013-9544-1

Jackson, C., Mohr-Schroeder, M., Bush, S., Maiorca, C., Roberts, T., Yost, C., & Fowler, A. (2021). Equity-oriented conceptual framework for K-12 STEM literacy. *International Journal of STEM Education, 8*, 1–16. https://doi.org/10.1186/s40594-021-00294-z

Jho, H., Hong, O., & Song, J. (2016). An Analysis of STEM/STEAM teacher education in Korea with a case study of two schools from a community of practice perspective. *Eurasia Journal of Mathematics, Science and Technology Education, 12*, 1843–1862. https://doi.org/10.12973/EURASIA.2016.1538A

Kim, H. Y., & Serrano, A. (2017). Enhancing critical visual literacy through illustrations in a picturebook. *WOW Stories, 5*(3), 13–27. https://wowlit.org/wp-content/media/WOW-Stories-V5-I3-Kim-and-Serrano-Article.pdf

Ladson-Billings, G. (1995). Toward a theory of culturally relevant pedagogy. *American Educational Research Journal, 32*(3), 465–491. https://doi.org/10.2307/1163320

Lee, O., & Buxton, C. A. (2010). *Diversity and equity in science education: Research, policy, and practice.* Multicultural Education Series. Teachers College Press.

Lee, O., Maerten-Rivera, J., Penfield, R. D., LeRoy, K., & Secada, W. G. (2008). Science achievement of English language learners in urban elementary schools: Results of a first-year professional development intervention. *Journal of Research in Science Teaching, 45*, 31–52.

Lin, C., & Tsai, C. (2020). The effect of a pedagogical STEAM model on students' project competence and learning motivation. *Journal of Science Education and Technology, 30*, 112–124. https://doi.org/10.1007/s10956-020-09885-x

Lucas, T., & Villegas, A. M. (2010). The missing piece in teacher education: The preparation of linguistically responsive teachers. *National Society for the Study of Education, 109*, 297–318.

Margolis, J., Estrella, R., Goode, J., Holme, J., & Nao, K. (2010). *Stuck in the shallow end: Education, race, and computing.* MIT Press.

Moldavan, A., & Gupta, D. (2024). Culturally relevant science learning. *Science and Children, 61*(1), 70–76. DOI:10.1080/00368148.2023.2292390

Moll, L., Amanti, C., Neff, D., & Gonzalez, N. (1992). Funds of knowledge for teaching: Using a qualitative approach to connect homes to classrooms. *Theory into Practice, 31*(2), 132–141.

National Academies of Sciences, Engineering, and Medicine (NASEM). (2018). *English learners in STEM subjects: Transforming classrooms, schools, and lives.* National Academies Press.

National Academies of Sciences, Engineering, and Medicine (NASEM). (2020). *Building capacity for teaching engineering in K–12 education.* National Academies Press. https://doi.org/10.17226/25612

National Academies of Sciences, Engineering, and Medicine (NASEM). (2022). *Science and engineering in preschool through elementary grades: The brilliance of children and the strengths of educators.* National Academies Press. https://doi.org/10.17226/26215

National Center for Educational Statistics. (2023). *English learners in public schools.* U.S. Department of Education, Institute of Education Sciences. https://nces.ed.gov/programs/coe/indicator/cgf

Newfield, D. (2011). From visual literacy to critical visual literacy: An analysis of educational materials. *English Teaching: Practice and Critique, 10*(1), 81–94. https://files.eric.ed.gov/fulltext/EJ935564.pdf

Poland, S., Colburn, A., & Long, D. (2017). Teacher perspectives on specialisation in the elementary classroom: Implications for science instruction. *International Journal of Science Education, 39,* 1715–1732. https://doi.org/10.1080/09500693.2017.1351646

Poza, L. E. (2016). The language of *ciencia*: Translanguaging and learning in a bilingual science classroom. *International Journal of Bilingual Education and Bilingualism, 21*(1), 1–19. DOI:10.1080/13670050.2015.1125849

Prain, V., & Waldrip, B. (2006). An exploratory study of teachers' and students' use of multi-modal representations of concepts in primary science. *International Journal of Science Education, 28,* 1843–1866. https://doi.org/10.1080/09500690600718294

Rainey, K., Dancy, M., & Mickelson, R. (2018). Race and gender differences in how sense of belonging influences decisions to major in STEM. *International Journal of STEM Education, 5*(10). https://doi.org/10.1186/s40594-018-0115-6

Ramsay-Jordan, N. (2020). Hidden figures: How pecuniary influences help shape STEM experiences for Black students in grades K-12. *Journal of Economics, Race, and Policy, 3,* 180–194. https://doi.org/10.1007/s41996-019-00049-7

Reider, D., Davis, N., & Nariman, N. (2021). *Problem-based learning increases STEM interest for high school students and instructors* [Conference presentation]. IAFOR International Conference on Education, Honolulu, HI, United States.

Riddle, B. (2021). Visual literacy—the 3Rs or STEAM? *Scope on the Skies, 44*(6), 93–99. https://www.nsta.org/science-scope/science-scope-julyaugust-2021-0/visual-literacy-3rs-or-steam

Roe, K. (2019). Supporting student assets and demonstrating respect for funds of knowledge. *Journal of Invitational Theory & Practice, 25,* 5–13.

Sanford, A. K., Pinkney, C. J., Brown, J. E., Elliott, C. G., Rotert, E. N., & Sennott, S. C. (2020). Culturally and linguistically responsive mathematics instruction for English learners in multitiered support systems: PLUSS enhancements. *Learning Disability Quarterly, 43*(2), 101–114.

Santa, C., Havens, L., & Valdes, B. (2004). *Project CRISS: Creating independence through student-owned strategies.* Kendall Hunt.

Santos Costa, G., & Xavier, A. C. (2016). Critical visual literacy: The new phase of applied linguistics in the era of mobile technology. In A. Pareja-Lora, C. Calle-Martínez & P. Rodríguez-Arancón (Eds.), *New perspectives on teaching and working with languages in the digital era* (pp. 201–212). Research-publishing.net. http://dx.doi.org/10.14705/rpnet.2016.tislid2014.434

Schallert, S., Lavicza, Z., & Vandervieren, E. (2021). Towards inquiry-based flipped classroom scenarios: A design heuristic and principles for lesson planning. *International Journal of Science and Mathematics Education, 20*, 277–297. https://doi.org/10.1007/s10763-021-10167-0

Shillingford, A., Oh, S., & Finnell, L. (2017). Promoting STEM career development among students and parents of color: Are school counselors leading the charge? *Professional School Counseling, 21*(1b), 1–11.

Torres-Velasquez, D., & Lobo, G. (2005). Research, reflection, and practice: Culturally responsive mathematics teaching and English language learners. *Teaching Children Mathematics, 11*(5), 249–255. https://doi.org/10.5951/TCM.11.5.0249

Vakil, S. (2018). Ethics, identity, and political vision: Toward a justice-centered approach to equity in computer science education. *Harvard Educational Review, 88*(1), 26–52.

Vielma, K. (2023). Building ethical awareness using culturally relevant practices in STEM departments. In E. Hildt, K. Laas, E. M. Brey & C. Z. Miller (Eds.), *Building inclusive ethical cultures in STEM* (pp. 163–176). Springer. DOI:10.1007/978-3-031-51560-6_10

Zimmerman, A. (2016). Developing confidence in STEAM: Exploring the challenges that novice elementary teachers face. *STEAM Journal, 2*, Article 15. https://doi.org/10.5642/steam.20160202.15

Part II

Application of the Framework

STEAM Learning Community

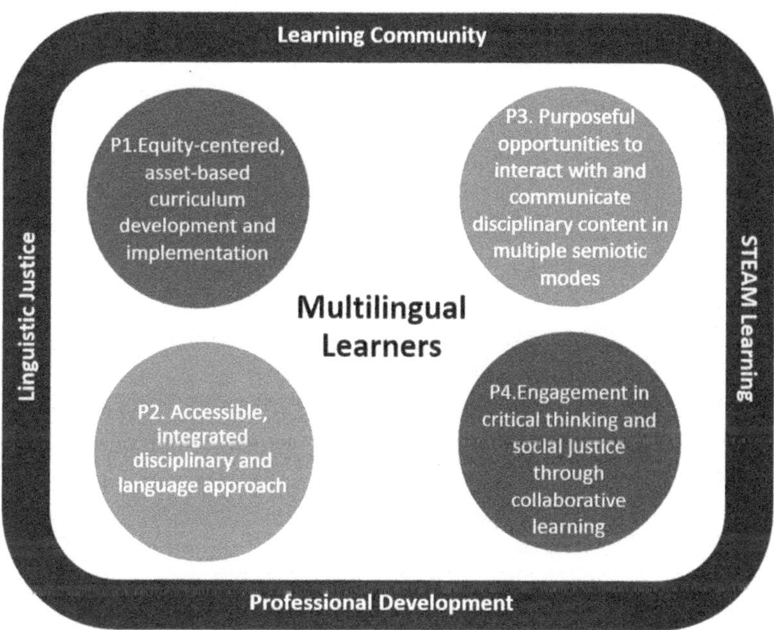

Figure 3.1 ESEM Framework

Ms. Young's school is located in a high-poverty neighborhood in Chicago (see Table 3.2 for class profile). The first graders were interested in animals and wildlife, but opportunities to interact with such were limited in the inner-city setting. However, the students frequently observed dead birds resulting from collisions with high-rise buildings in the city of Chicago. Recognizing the resources in the STEAM learning community and the importance of connecting learning to real-world issues, Ms. Young

Table 3.1 Focused Core Principles and Key Practices in ESEM Framework

Focused Core Principles	Key Teaching Practices
P1. Equity-centered, asset-based curriculum development and implementation	P1.1 Ensure that curriculum content is relevant, inclusive, and accessible to all students. P1.2 Design learning units that are informed by standards and critical issues in the local and global communities. P1.3 Develop learning experiences that reflect and build on the cultural and linguistic assets of MLs and diverse disciplinary practices. P1.4 Provide opportunities for MLs to see themselves reflected positively in the curriculum and learning environment. P1.5 Implement teaching strategies that recognize and value MLs' linguistic and cultural assets.
P4. Engagement in critical thinking and social justice through collaborative learning	P4.1 Foster a classroom culture that respects each other, values critical thinking, and builds community. P4.2 Encourage MLs to critically examine issues of power, privilege, and inequality in a disciplinary context. P4.3 Facilitate collaborative learning experiences that promote critical inquiry, evaluate multiple perspectives, and build empathy. P4.4 Provide opportunities for MLs to generate evidence-based arguments on social justice topics, drawing on their diverse cultural perspectives and experiences. P4.5 Encourage MLs to take action on social justice issues that have impact on their communities, promoting agency and advocacy.

decided to create and implement a "Saving Birds" STEAM unit. By showing images of migrating bird collision incidents (e.g., https://www.nytimes.com/2023/10/08/us/birds-dead-chicago-building.html), organizing a visit to the Field Museum, and prompting students to brainstorm solutions, Ms. Young not only engaged her students but also fostered empathy and environmental awareness. Through these hands-on projects, she cultivated a love for science while instilling a sense of responsibility toward wildlife and the environment. Concluding the project with social actions, Ms. Young tasked students with writing letters or making drawings to send to

Table 3.2 Class Profile 1

Context	Urban inner-city, high-poverty community, 1st grade, transitional bilingual program where English and Spanish are used for instruction
Teachers	**Ms. Young**, a bilingual Spanish and English teacher

Selected ML Profiles	**Jose**
	• Born in the US to first-generation immigrant parents from Mexico.
	• **Spanish**
	  ◦ Oracy: developing
	  ◦ Literacy: entering
	• **English**
	  ◦ Oracy: emerging
	  ◦ Literacy: emerging
	
	Lyla
	• Born in the US to first-generation Arab American parents.
	• **Arabic**
	  ◦ Oracy: developing
	  ◦ Literacy: entering
	• **English**
	  ◦ Oracy: expanding
	  ◦ Literacy: emerging
	• **Spanish**
	  ◦ Oracy: emerging
	  ◦ Literacy: entering

city officials, outlining their findings and suggesting measures to prevent bird collisions with high-rise buildings.

A sneak peek of Ms. Young's classroom at the beginning of the chapter prompts the question of how the STEAM learning community plays a role in shaping curriculum and instruction. In this chapter, we explore the concept of the STEAM learning community and its connection with the core principles of the ESEM Framework. Further, we offer three practical tools to establish an inclusive STEAM learning community. We conclude the chapter by revisiting Ms. Young's classroom, seeing how she applied these tools to foster an inclusive STEAM learning community and develop and implement an equitable and asset-based curriculum. The companion website provides additional resources related to the topics in this chapter.

What Is the STEAM Learning Community?

The STEAM learning community is one of the four "sides" surrounding and strengthening the core principles in our framework. Envisioning the STEAM learning community through the analogy of an ecosystem can provide valuable insights. Like a natural ecosystem, the STEAM learning community consists of interconnected components that collaboratively facilitate the progress toward a shared goal. We will examine the STEAM learning community (see Figure 3.2) through the lenses of "habitats" and "species."

The "habitats" of the STEAM learning community are the local and global communities in which our MLs and their families are deeply rooted. These "habitats" provide nourishment, essential resources, and safety to the "species" growing and thriving within them. Because many ML families have experiences living in another countries, both the local and global communities serve as the "habitats" that inform curriculum planning and implementation.

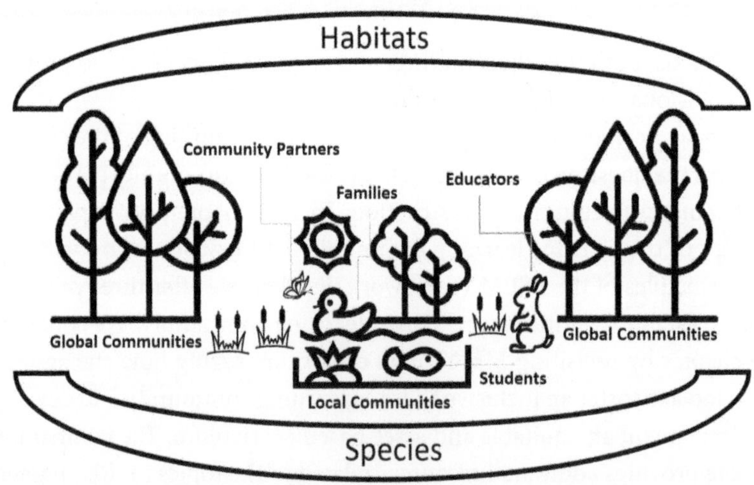

Figure 3.2 Ecosystem of the STEAM Learning Community

Just as different species coexist and interact within an ecosystem, various stakeholders, such as students, families, educators, administrators, and community partners, are the "species" collaborating within the STEAM learning community. Our understanding of the learning community in the ESEM Framework is broadly defined, but we primarily focus on MLs and educators, including classroom teachers and all school staff, in this chapter. The partnership with families and community partners will be further explored in Chapter 6. In the ecosystem of the STEAM learning community, educators act as one of the primary "species," playing a crucial role in maintaining the balance. All students represent another primary "species," contributing their unique perspectives, talents, and learning styles to the ecosystem.

What Is the Role of the STEAM Learning Community in the ESEM Framework?

In this section, we will demonstrate how the STEAM learning community provides context to and enriches the key principles in the framework. While all the principles are intricately connected to the STEAM learning community, we will elaborate on two of the most relevant principles highlighted in Figure 3.1. These principles are P1: Developing and implementing equity-centered, asset-based curriculum; and P4: Engaging in critical thinking and social justice through collaborative learning (see details in Table 3.1).

Principle 1 aims at placing the funds of knowledge from MLs and their communities at the center of curriculum planning and implementation, thereby ensuring equity in STEAM education. The approach educators adopt in establishing the STEAM learning community plays a pivotal role in supporting this principle.

Rather than labeling MLs as deficient in English, educators recognize their linguistic proficiency and knowledge as valuable assets. Consequently, they integrate MLs' diverse linguistic practices to enrich disciplinary content. For example, there are numerous cognates related to STEAM between Latin-based languages and English (e.g., *animals* in English and *animales* in Spanish), which share similar spelling, pronunciation, and meanings in both languages. Explicitly supporting MLs to leverage these cognates can greatly enhance their understanding of STEAM concepts and content in English while simultaneously reinforcing their proficiency in their primary language. Further, it is essential to acknowledge that linguistic resources extend beyond vocabulary alone. MLs who are literate in their primary language can also transfer various literacy skills, such as making inferences, to a new language. Educators are encouraged to actively integrate MLs' primary languages and explicitly teach them how to leverage linguistic resources to enhance the learning of key STEAM concepts and content in English.

Moreover, MLs' rich cultural resources hold significant value and can positively contribute to enriching STEAM teaching and learning. For instance, MLs with lived experiences in various parts of the world, such as a rural community in Mexico or Bangladesh, may possess extensive knowledge about weather patterns and agricultural practices (e.g., floating gardens). Conversely, other MLs might have firsthand experience with environmental issues in metropolitan areas, such as pollution and heat islands. As highlighted in Chapter 1, the majority of MLs in our classrooms are US born and have resided in the local community for their entire lives. Therefore, cultural and ethnic diversity, as well as resources like community centers, local public libraries, museums, and parks within the local community, are equally significant contributors to STEAM education.

The STEAM learning community also plays a crucial role in supporting Principle 4: Engaging in critical thinking and social justice through collaborative learning. This principle significantly contributes to the overarching goal of equity and social justice in STEAM education by equipping all students and their families with essential critical thinking and problem-solving skills while activating their agency to advocate for meaningful changes in the local and global communities.

To implement Principle 4, educators can establish an inclusive learning community that values and honors each individual's languages, cultures, learning preferences, and interests. This can be accomplished by (1) creating a welcoming learning environment; (2) organizing community-building activities; and (3) fostering inquiry through critical analysis and evaluation of multiple perspectives and power dynamics embedded in STEAM-related phenomena or issues.

First of all, entering a new school in a new community can be an intimidating experience, let alone entering a school in a new country where the official language differs from one's native tongue. Establishing a welcoming learning environment, both socially and academically, is crucial. Examples of creating a welcoming social environment include displaying national flags representing the home countries of MLs, posting signage in the languages spoken by MLs, showcasing cultural artifacts, providing multilingual resources and personnel to welcome and support MLs and their families, and celebrating MLs' important ethnic holidays at the school.

In terms of fostering a welcoming learning environment from an academic perspective, some sample ideas include:

- Providing MLs with access to and support for engaging with the curriculum without watering down its rigor
- Positioning MLs and their families as valuable members whose knowledge and perspectives are essential for enhancing learning
- Facilitating open communication between home and school, with mitigation strategies and services in place to break down language barriers or cultural misunderstandings

Second, various community-building activities can be employed to support the creation of an inclusive learning community. One such activity revolves around the exploration of names, given that names from different languages may contain sounds unfamiliar to English-dominant speakers. A common practice for MLs and their families is to sacrifice their ethnic names and adopt Anglo names to facilitate pronunciation or fit in better. Further, naming conventions can differ significantly across cultures. "It's All in a Name" (Short et al., 2018) is an exemplary community-building activity designed to instill pride and respect for the names and cultures of MLs. Ideally done at the start of the school year, this activity encourages all members to share the pronunciation, meaning, significance, and origin of their names.

In addition to cultivating a welcoming learning environment and engaging in community-building activities, the third and final point is that STEAM educators are encouraged to place a strong emphasis on fostering critical inquiry in the learning community. Critical inquiry entails providing all students with opportunities and support to construct evidence-based arguments by analyzing and evaluating multiple perspectives within social, historical, cultural, and political contexts. Most importantly, critical inquiry empowers students to uncover the power dynamics embedded in the central phenomena or issues, encourages reflection on how they can activate their agency and advocate for changes, and promotes taking actions toward equity and social justice. An example of critical inquiry in Ms. Young's class is when students send their letters or drawings to city officials, prompting them to take actions to save birds.

What Are the Tools to Build the Inclusive STEAM Learning Community?

We have discussed what a STEAM learning community means and how it connects to the key principles in the framework. Next, we will introduce three sample tools that help educators establish an inclusive STEAM learning community. These three tools are:

- Multilingual learner (ML) profile
- STEAM asset mapping
- Equitable STEAM infrastructure

Multilingual Learner Profile

With a focus on exemplary teaching of English learners, Short et al. (2018) recommend that getting to know students as unique individuals be the top priority. As discussed in Chapter 1, MLs come from many different cultural and linguistic backgrounds. The selected multilingual student profiles in the classroom vignette also elaborate on how diverse these students' lived experiences and perspectives are. How do educators start to create a holistic ML profile that documents the dynamic use of languages?

To answer this question, educators need to gather as much information about their MLs as possible. There are various methods educators can employ to gather information for the ML profile. By collaborating with

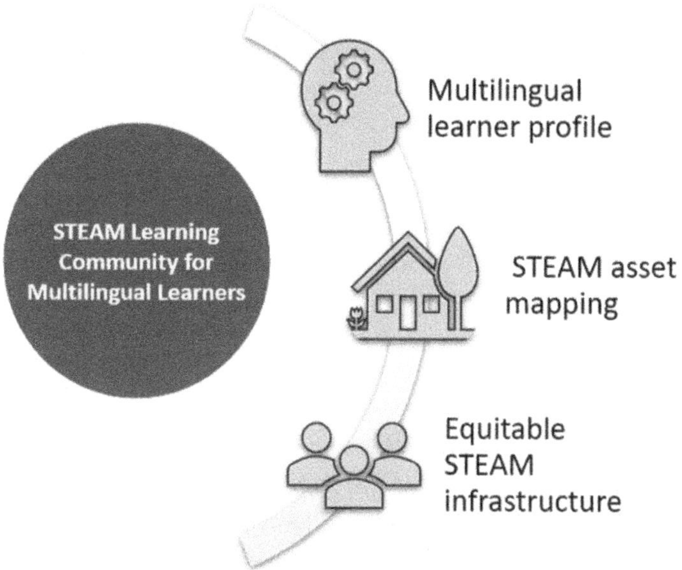

Figure 3.3 Tools for Establishing an Inclusive STEAM Learning Community for MLs

administrators and staff, teachers can utilize intake protocols developed by state agencies or the school district, along with the district's or state's home language survey and local or state language assessments, to collect and disseminate information about the MLs (Short et al., 2018).

Moreover, further inquiries about MLs' profiles are needed as some multilingual families may not indicate their home language practices other than English on the language survey due to the stigma associated with the label "English learners" (García et al., 2016). Such inquiries may include researching about MLs' home country and cultures through online resources, conducting home visits and family interviews, and facilitating class projects that offer valuable insights into MLs' cultures, languages, and lived experiences. We provide a list of sample interview questions, adapted from García et al. (2016), that educators can use to collaborate with MLs and their families to gather information for the ML profiles.

- Name of the ML student and pronunciation:
- Country(ies)/region(s) where the student has lived/visited since birth:

- Educational background:

  1) Education in English (indicate the country[ies] or region[s])

  2) Education in language(s) other than English (indicate the country[ies] or region[s])

- Language and literacy practices:

  1) Language(s) exposed to outside of school (e.g., home, friends, extended family in other country[ies] or region[s])

  2) Home language(s) and literacy:

  How well does the student speak and listen in home language(s)—Proficiency levels in speaking/listening:
  How well does the student read and write in home language(s)—Proficiency levels in reading/writing:

  3) Additional language(s) and literacy

  How well does the student speak and listen in additional language(s)—Proficiency levels in speaking/listening:
  How well does the student read and write in additional language(s)—Proficiency levels in reading/writing:

- Significant events during childhood that may impact learning (at home or related to the country of origin):

Another method for gathering information for ML profiles is a class project like the multimodal "Who Am I?" digital storytelling activity, which allows students to develop a digital narrative using images, narration, music, and text to share their identities and experiences. Engaging in inquiries across various sources to gather cultural and linguistic resources for the ML profile is one of the essential tools for establishing an inclusive STEAM learning community.

STEAM Asset Mapping

STEAM asset mapping is the second tool for establishing an equity-centered STEAM learning community. It plays a pivotal role by identifying and leveraging the resources, strengths, and opportunities within communities to create inclusive and empowering learning experiences. Through this process, educators can systematically assess the existing STEAM assets, including community organizations, cultural institutions, local experts, and available technologies, to inform curriculum design and delivery. By recognizing and valuing the diverse knowledge, skills, and cultural backgrounds presented within the community, asset-based curriculum development ensures that learning experiences are relevant, meaningful, and responsive to the needs and interests of all students, particularly those from historically marginalized or underrepresented groups. Furthermore, by engaging stakeholders, such as students, families, community members, and industry partners, in the asset mapping process, educators can cultivate collaborative relationships and co-create learning opportunities that reflect the richness and diversity of the local community.

For example, the Argonne National Laboratory initiated a STEM asset mapping project in 2022 that provides educators with valuable STEAM asset information on Chicago's South Side (https://www.anl.gov/reference/argonne-in-chicago-stem-asset-mapping-project). Through engagement with stakeholders, this project identifies and utilizes existing STEM resources to prompt equitable access and address systemic barriers to participation. By mapping educational programs, technological infrastructure, and community organizations, the program empowers marginalized residents to engage in STEAM activities, enhancing community resilience and inclusivity. This approach can be adopted in different school communities, utilizing tools like a geographic information system (GIS) to visualize local assets, identify collaboration opportunities, and enrich educational experiences (e.g., GIS for schools, https://www.esri.com/en-us/industries/k-12-education/overview).

Equitable STEAM Infrastructure

The third tool we introduce is equitable STEAM infrastructure, which not only benefits students but also extends to STEAM personnel, including teachers, administrators, and support staff. By participating in professional development opportunities focused on culturally and linguistically responsive teaching strategies, STEAM educators can better meet the needs of MLs in their schools. This training empowers educators to create inclusive learning environments where all students feel valued and supported, regardless of their language background.

Additionally, equitable infrastructure ensures that educators have access to resources and tools that facilitate effective instruction for MLs, such

Table 3.3 Template for STEAM Learning Community and Applications for Curriculum and Instruction

Synthesis and Application	ML Profile	STEAM Asset Mapping	Equitable STEAM Infrastructure
	• What is the background of the student and family? • What is the student's educational background? • How does the student engage in language and literacy practices both within and outside of the school? • What are significant events that have played a role in shaping the student's identity?	• How can we acknowledge and celebrate contributions that have been historically excluded? • How is diverse representation of personnel reflected in the STEAM asset mapping? • In what ways are STEAM resources utilized to promote equity? • How does community engagement align with an equity lens in STEAM initiatives?	• What are barriers that affect MLs' access to STEAM programs and resources within STEAM infrastructure? • How are professional development programs tailored to meet identified needs? • What types of curriculum and instruction resources are available to support STEAM education? • How are community partnerships established and maintained to enhance STEAM initiatives?

Assets and resources from
MLs, families, school, local
communities, and global
communities

Support in place to ensure equity
and social justice in STEAM
education

Unit topic

Standards

Outcome/impact to share with
students and families (provide
the information in MLs' primary
language)

Instructional activities

as translated materials, language interpretation services, and technology platforms that support multilingual learning. Moreover, by diversifying the teaching staff and encouraging collaboration among them, schools can further enhance the cultural relevance and responsiveness of STEAM education. By investing in the professional growth and support of STEAM personnel, equitable infrastructure strengthens the capacity of educators to effectively engage and empower MLs in STEAM learning, leading to improved outcomes for all stakeholders.

In this section, we have introduced and elaborated on three essential tools to establish an inclusive STEAM learning community for MLs. Table 3.3 provides a template that synthesizes how these tools can be used cohesively to inform equity-focused, asset-centered curriculum development and instruction.

What Does the Application of the STEAM Learning Community Tools Look Like?

Equipped with various tools to build an inclusive STEAM learning community, educators can apply them in curriculum development and instruction to create equity- and justice-focused STEAM education for MLs. Returning to the beginning vignette of the chapter, we illustrate how Ms. Young, the first-grade teacher, utilized these tools and synthesized the information to inform the development and delivery of the STEAM unit "Saving Birds."

Ms. Young created ML profiles for both Jose and Lyla by gathering relevant information. Born and growing up in first-generation immigrant households, Jose and Lyla attended public schools since kindergarten in the United States. In terms of language and literacy practices, Jose and Lyla are learning Spanish and English through the transitional bilingual program at school. Living in first-generation immigrant households, Jose and Lyla are regularly exposed to the primary language of the family. In Jose's case, this is Spanish. For Lyla, it is Arabic. The primary languages are used to communicate daily routines, family activities, religion, and news and events from their home country. In addition to using primary language to maintain connections with their extended families and fulfill basic needs while visiting their home country, they use the language to communicate with friends from the local community who share the same ethnic background.

Ms. Young used information gathered from home language surveys, family interviews, and available school data to create the holistic ML profiles that document the proficiency levels of all the languages Jose and Lyla use and their family backgrounds.

ML profiles from class vignette:

Jose
- Born in the US to first-generation immigrant parents from Mexico.
- **Spanish**
  - Oracy: developing
  - Literacy: entering
- **English**
  - Oracy: emerging
  - Literacy: emerging

Lyla
- Born in the US to first-generation Arabic American parents.
- **Arabic**
  - Oracy: developing
  - Literacy: entering
- **English**
  - Oracy: expanding
  - Literacy: emerging
- **Spanish**
  - Oracy: emerging
  - Literacy: entering

The ML profiles also included MLs' cultural knowledge about the topic. Ms. Young investigated the cultural connections Arabic and Mexican cultures have with birds and discovered that in both cultures, birds hold symbolic significance, representing freedom and beauty. Birds frequently appear in various artistic representations, including Mexican folk art and crafts, as well as in Arabic calligraphy. Known for their migratory patterns, birds fly across continents and borders. This natural behavior may resonate with children from immigrant households, as the idea of birds migrating to find new habitats or opportunities could mirror the experiences of MLs' families seeking new lives in Chicago.

The second tool utilized by Ms. Young is STEAM asset mapping. Growing up in a high-poverty, inner-city community of Chicago, Jose and Lyla experience firsthand the challenges their parents face in making ends meet. Furthermore, their school struggles with insufficient resources to provide essential learning tools and retain qualified teaching staff. Despite the students' interest in the natural world and animals, the urban environment limits opportunities to explore such topics.

However, metropolitan Chicago boasts abundant community resources, including its iconic skyline featuring skyscrapers, towers, and landmarks, as well as world-class museums. Additionally, local communities are home to experts from diverse cultural backgrounds, such as ornithologists and architects from the University of Chicago, whose knowledge and experiences could enrich the school's STEAM education and support initiatives and actions toward equity and social justice. Most importantly, Chicago offers various bird conservatories, sanctuaries, organizations, and activities (see Figure 3.4). Additionally, the community partner the Field Museum offers free field trips for students from low-socioeconomic-status schools. Ms. Young was able to register for a free field trip through the museum's community outreach program (https://www.fieldmuseum. org/register-your-field-trip-group). She brought her class to explore the bird exhibits at the museum.

As for equitable STEAM infrastructure, the needs assessment revealed that there were some bilingual (Spanish and English) resources available for MLs such as Jose and their families. However, teaching resources and school personnel proficient in languages other than Spanish and English were very scarce. Furthermore, the transitional bilingual program kept Spanish and English on a self-contained schedule, thereby providing limited opportunities for MLs to use translanguaging for academic purposes. While all teachers had the opportunity to participate in professional development centered on culturally responsive teaching, those working in the transitional bilingual program were also able to attend virtual webinars hosted by the state education resource center. These webinars explored translanguaging strategies and provided long-term support for MLs' primary languages after they exited the program.

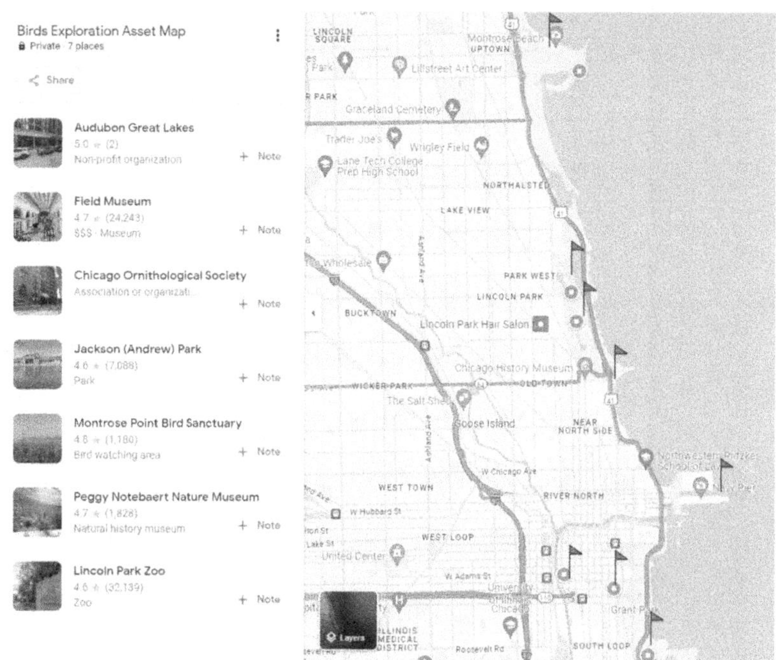

Figure 3.4 Bird Conservatories and Activities in Chicago

Table 3.4 shows how Ms. Young applied the three recommended tools to establish an inclusive STEAM learning community and implement the equitable and asset-based approach for STEAM instruction. The details are provided below using the 5E model.

Engage: Ms. Young began by capturing students' attention and interest in STEAM through a compelling story with a photo. She showed images of birds in the city (see an example in Figure 3.5). The real-world scenario of birds in the city colliding with buildings prompted students to recognize the significance of the issue and stimulated their curiosity about birds and their habitats. She asked the students why it happened and how to prevent bird collisions. Students came up with possible solutions and narrowed these down to testable ideas. Students decided to test out their initial ideas.

Explore: Next, Ms. Young organized a field trip to the Field Museum, providing students with a hands-on exploration of bird specimens and related exhibits. This immersive experience allowed students to observe and interact with real-life examples of birds, deepening their understanding of avian biology and behavior. Through guided activities

Table 3.4 Applying STEAM Learning Community Tools to Inform Curriculum and Instruction

Synthesis and Application	ML Profile	STEAM Asset Mapping	Equitable STEAM Infrastructure
	• What is the student and family's background? • What is the student's educational background? • How does the student engage in language and literacy practices both within and outside of the school? • What are significant events that have played a role in shaping the student's identity?	• How can we acknowledge and celebrate contributions that have been historically excluded? • How is diverse representation of personnel reflected in the STEAM asset mapping? • In what ways are STEAM resources utilized to promote equity? • How does community engagement align with an equity lens in STEAM initiatives?	• What are barriers that affect MLs' access to STEAM programs and resources within STEAM infrastructure? • How are professional development programs tailored to meet identified needs? • What types of curriculum and instruction resources are available to support STEAM education? • How are community partnerships established and maintained to enhance STEAM initiatives?
Assets and resources from MLs, families, school, local communities, and global communities	Linguistic and cultural assets from MLs and families Content experts from the local and global communities Resources in different languages Community resources related to the topic		

Support in place to ensure equity and social justice in STEAM education	Transitional bilingual program, bilingual teachers, and bilingual resources at school Free access to the Field Museum Standard-based, student-centered curriculum development and implementation that leverage and expand MLs' linguistic and cultural assets
Unit topic	Saving Birds
Standards	**Performance Expectation:** 1-LS1-1 Use materials to design a solution to a human problem by mimicking how plants and/or animals use their external parts to help them survive, grow, and meet their needs **DCI:** 1.LS1.A Structure and Function **SEP:** Constructing explanations and designing solutions **CCC:** Structure and function **NOS:** Science knowledge is based on empirical evidence.
Outcome/impact to share with students and families	Students will be able to construct explanations and design solutions to help save migrating birds from collisions with high-rise buildings in Chicago, understanding the structure and function of both birds and buildings (in English). Los estudiantes construirán explicaciones y diseñarán soluciones para ayudar a salvar a las aves migratorias de las colisiones con los edificios altos en Chicago, entendiendo la estructura y función tanto de las aves como de los edificios (in Spanish).
Instructional activities	5E learning cycle

Figure 3.5 Birds in the City

ZeroOne. (2008). *Feral pigeons on the Empire State Building.* https://commons.
wikimedia.org/wiki/File:Feral_pigeon_-Empire_State_Building,_New_York_City,_
USA-31Aug2008d.jpg

and observations, students began to make connections between their classroom learning and the broader scientific concepts presented at the museum. Additionally, students engaged in visual data analysis with maps and graphs, examining migration patterns and collision hot spots to further understand the issue.

Explain: Following the museum visit, Ms. Young guided students in reflecting on their observations and experiences. She asked students to share their thoughts and insights, facilitating discussion about the challenges faced by migrating birds and the factors contributing to bird collisions with buildings. Through these discussions, students developed a deeper understanding of the issues at hand and began to formulate potential solutions.

Elaborate: With a solid foundation of knowledge and understanding, students engaged in hands-on activities and projects designed to further explore the topic of bird conservation. Ms. Young encouraged students to brainstorm creative solutions to prevent bird collisions with high-rise buildings, fostering critical thinking and problem-solving skills. Through art projects, research assignments, and collaborative activities, students deepened their appreciation for the importance of protecting wildlife and preserving their habitats.

Evaluate: Finally, Ms. Young assessed students' learning and understanding of the topic. She tasked students with writing letters or sending drawings to city officials, articulating their findings, and proposing actionable measures to mitigate bird collisions with high-rise buildings. This assignment allowed students to demonstrate their comprehension of the issue and their ability to apply scientific knowledge to real-world problems, empowering them to become advocates for environmental conservation.

Conclusion

This chapter highlights the pivotal role of the STEAM learning community in reinforcing and enhancing the core principles in the ESEM framework. By conceptualizing the STEAM learning community as an ecosystem, educators gain insight into the interconnected nature of its components. The learning community thrives on the presence of diverse "habitats" such as local and global communities, which protect and nourish their "species," including students, educators, families, and community partners. Collaboration among these components is key to fostering a welcoming learning environment. Importantly, changes within one aspect of the ecosystem can have ripple effects that impact the entire system and beyond.

Furthermore, we introduce three practical tools designed to support educators in cultivating an inclusive STEAM learning community: creating ML profiles, mapping community assets, and establishing equitable infrastructure. These tools offer tangible strategies for empowering educators to tailor their approach to meet the diverse needs of their students. To illustrate the application of these tools in practice, we present the class vignette featuring Ms. Young, a first-grade teacher, who utilized them to develop and implement a STEAM unit "Saving Birds." Through her example, we demonstrate how these tools can be effectively integrated into STEAM curriculum development and instruction to promote equitable learning experiences for all learners.

References

García, O., Johnson, S. I., & Seltzer, K. (2016). *The translanguaging classroom.* Brookes.

Short, D., Becker, H., Cloud, N., Hellman, A. B., Levine, L. N., & Cummins, J. (2018). *The 6 principles for exemplary teaching of English learners: Grades K-12.* TESOL International.

ZeroOne. (2008). *Feral pigeons on the Empire State Building.* https://commons.wikimedia.org/wiki/File:Feral_pigeon_-Empire_State_Building,_New_York_City,_USA-31Aug2008d.jpg

4

Curriculum Development, Implementation, and Assessment in STEAM Education

Vishodana Thamotharan

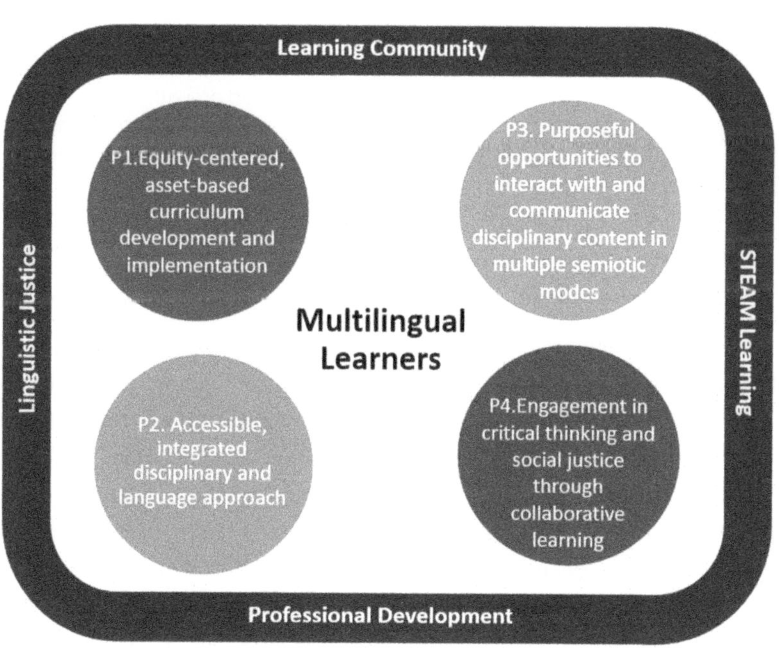

Figure 4.1 ESEM Framework

Table 4.1 Focused Core Principles and Key Practices in ESEM Framework

Focused Core Principles	Key Teaching Practices
P1. Equity-centered, asset-based curriculum development and implementation	P1.1 Ensure that curriculum content is relevant, inclusive, and accessible to all students. P1.2 Design learning units that are informed by standards and critical issues in the local and global communities. P1.3 Develop learning experiences that reflect and build on the cultural and linguistic assets of MLs and diverse disciplinary practices. P1.4 Provide opportunities for MLs to see themselves reflected positively in the curriculum and learning environment. P1.5 Implement teaching strategies that recognize and value MLs' linguistic and cultural assets.
P4. Engagement in critical thinking and social justice through collaborative learning	P4.1 Foster a classroom culture that respects each other, values critical thinking, and builds community. P4.2 Encourage MLs to critically examine issues of power, privilege, and inequality in a disciplinary context. P4.3 Facilitate collaborative learning experiences that promote critical inquiry, evaluate multiple perspectives, and build empathy. P4.4 Provide opportunities for MLs to generate evidence-based arguments on social justice topics, drawing on their diverse cultural perspectives and experiences. P4.5 Encourage MLs to take action on social justice issues that have impact on their communities, promoting agency and advocacy.

As is true at many schools, Ms. Nowak's schedule offered science twice a week for 30 minutes and art once a week for 45 minutes during specials. Ms. Nowak noticed her students were most interested and engaged during science and art, so she wanted to find a creative way to integrate them into her schedule that was predominantly math and English language arts (ELA). She decided to do a project-based learning (PBL) unit. The approach allowed her to teach her students science concepts while concurrently addressing Common Core ELA and math standards. She started with choosing a problem most relevant to her students: loss of farming land, a topic that students who grew up in the community were

Table 4.2 Class Profile 3

Context	Rural, 5th grade, content-based language instruction model
Teacher	**Ms. Nowak**, a Polish and English bilingual speaker who immigrated with her family to the US in her teen years

Selected ML Profiles	**Allin**
	• Born in Angola with Umbundu- and Portuguese-speaking parents. The family moved to the US when she was four years old. Allin is at risk of becoming a long-term English learner (L-TEL).
	• **Umbundu**
	  ○ Oracy: developing
	  ○ Literacy: entering
	• **Portuguese**
	  ○ Oracy: developing
	  ○ Literacy: entering
	• **English**
	  ○ Oracy: bridging
	  ○ Literacy: developing
	
	Mario
	• Born in Venezuela and had interrupted schooling while the family fled political turmoil and economic collapse before immigrating to the US. Mario is considered a student with interrupted or limited formal education (SIFE).
	• **Spanish**
	  ○ Oracy: developing
	  ○ Literacy: entering
	• **English**
	  ○ Oracy: expanding
	  ○ Literacy: developing

very familiar with and an issue they heard their families often discuss. Before she committed to the idea, Ms. Nowak wanted to understand Mario's and Allin's experiences with rural communities, so she asked the students (see Figure 4.2, Step 1). She learned that while Mario was not from a rural community, Mario's mother developed a community garden. Additionally, Mario's father worked with imports and exports, and so Mario saw a change in the vegetation being exported. Allin had less experience with agriculture because her home country, Angola, makes agricultural activities difficult to engage in despite its expansive agricultural landscape. Ms. Nowak decided to focus on eco-friendly farming because she could not only help her students understand and support the local community but also draw on the experiences of Mario's and Allin's families to discuss global justice issues and solutions.

Guiding Questions for Unit Planning: Starting a PBL unit for MLs can appear overwhelming. Below are some guiding questions to support teachers as they plan and implement PBL for MLs.

PBL Focus:

1. How does this standard connect to my students' lives?
2. With what aspects of this topic do my students have agency?
3. Why is this topic of importance to my students (beyond just relevance)?
4. What are the justice-focused aspects of the topic?

Culturally and Linguistically Responsive Focus:

1. What are my students' needs?
2. What are my students' linguistic and cultural assets that I can leverage?
3. What tools do I need to support my students in determining a question?
4. What tools do I need to support my students in designing their process?
5. How can I support my students in sharing their project?
6. What checkpoints should I include to assess and guide my students?

How Do We Design the STEAM Curriculum?

Designing a STEAM curriculum requires intentional planning from the teacher. Teachers need to consider how they will teach each content area while also supporting students in making connections across content areas in meaningful ways. This requires connection to self and real-world spaces, to co-creating learning, inquiry, and opportunities to apply their learning to support the community. By allowing students to see themselves in the STEAM curriculum while also making the STEAM learning actionable, students understand that they have agency and opportunities for advocacy in and through STEAM.

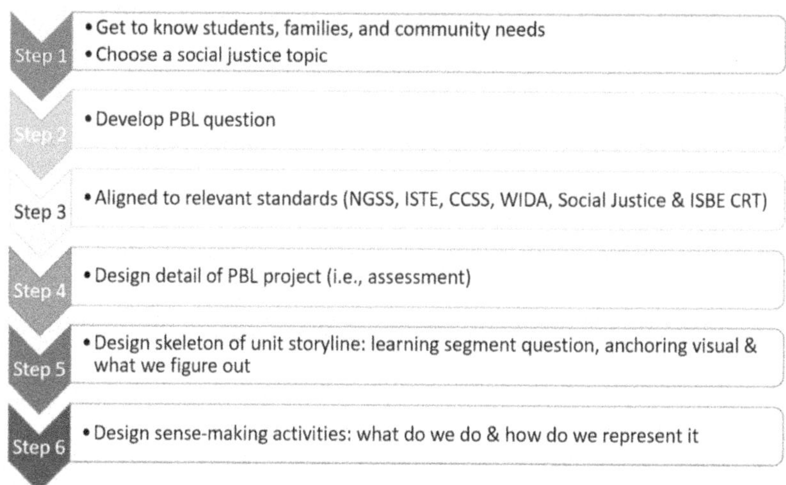

Figure 4.2 Steps to Planning a STEAM Unit

In the example of Ms. Nowak, her focus on eco-friendly farming is a social justice STEAM topic that has both local and global connections. Additionally, she chose "How can we design an eco-friendly community that meets the needs of our community while protecting the environment?" as her challenge question of the unit (see Figure 4.2, Step 2). Inherent to the question is the need for students to think about their own role as change agents and advocates for their community.

Standards Alignment

Following the Understanding by Design backward planning model, STEAM curriculum is planned with the end in mind (Wiggins & McTighe, 2012). First, the teacher identifies the standards (see Figure 4.2, Step 3). STEAM curriculum should align to national standards: Next Generation Science Standards (NGSS), International Standards for Technology Education (ISTE), National Core Art Standards (NCAS), Common Core State Standards in Mathematics (CCSS), World-Class Instructional Design and Assessment (WIDA), Teaching for Social Justice Standards (SJS), and state standards (e.g., Illinois State Board of Education Culturally Responsive Teaching and Leading Standards [CRTL]). In Ms. Nowak's example, the following is a sample set of standards she chose:

NGSS:

5-PS1-2: Measure and graph quantities to provide evidence that regardless of the type of change that occurs when heating, cooling, or mixing substances, the total weight of matter is conserved.

5-PS1-4: Conduct an investigation to determine whether the mixing of two or more substances results in new substances.

5-ESS3: Obtain and combine information about ways individual communities use science ideas to protect the Earth's resources and environment.

3-5 ETS1: Generate and compare multiple solutions to a problem based on how well each is likely to meet the criteria and constraints of the problem.

ISTE:

1.4.a Design Process: Students know and use a deliberate design process for generating ideas, testing theories, creating innovative artifacts or solving authentic problems.

NCAS:

VA:Cr1.1.5a: Combine ideas to generate an innovative idea for art-making.

CCSS:

5. MD.A.1: Convert among different sized standard measurement units with a given measurement system.

5. MD.B.2: Make a line plot to display a data set of measurements in fractions of a unit.

MP. 4: Model with mathematics.

WIDA:

ELD-MA.4-5: Interpret mathematics arguments by comparing conjectures with patterns, and/or rules.

ELD-SC.4-5: Interpret scientific explanations by obtaining and combining evidence and information to help explain how or why a phenomenon occurs.

SJS:

ID.3-5.5: I know my family and I do things the same as and different from other people and groups, and I know how to use what I learn from home, school, and other places that matter to me.

CRTL:

A.4: Include representative, familiar content in the curriculum to legitimize students' backgrounds while also exposing them to new ideas and worldviews different from their own.

E.6 Research and offer student advocacy content with real-world implications.

F.11: Collaborate effectively over time with the local community and community agencies, when and where appropriate, to promote a positive environment for student learning.

Assessment

Continuing with the Understanding by Design model, teachers need to consider how the students will be assessed at the end of the unit prior to choosing unit activities (see Figure 4.2, Step 4). This is particularly important because it will help the teacher be intentional in planning around the necessary skills and knowledge needed to successfully complete the assessment.

As stated earlier, Ms. Nowak is using project-based learning (PBL). PBL is designed around a public product that will address a challenging question or problem. This product serves as the assessment for the unit. PBLWorks suggests that once students complete their project, they should share it with partners who have a meaningful interest in the topic. While PBL does not require a social justice topic, it does encourage authentic public action. In Ms. Nowak's case, her students would design a component of an eco-friendly community that addresses the needs of their community while protecting the environment and explain their reasoning. They could choose to share their product with local farmers, the town council, or other stakeholders. In this way, the public product is the enactment of their agency.

Designing the Learning Process

The Process

Designing the process of learning requires attention to the details—both in what students should know (content) as well as be able to do (practices). At the same time, the process of learning should be driven by student curiosity—student questions. In science education, Ambitious Science Teaching (AST) is utilized to support students' ongoing thinking. Similar to the process of Ms. Nowak's example above, AST begins with a phenomenon or an event or process that interests students (Ambitious

Science Teaching, n.d.). Throughout the curriculum, the teacher's role is to elicit student ideas, support ongoing changes in student thinking via sense-making activities, and promote evidence-based reasoning (Ambitious Science Teaching, n.d.).

To center and guide the unit around student questions, the Next Generation Science Storyline approach is utilized (see Figure 4.2, Steps 5 and 6). "A storyline is a coherent sequence of lessons, in which each step is driven by students' questions that arise from their interactions with phenomena" (Next Generation Science Storylines, n.d.). As students learn more about the phenomenon, they explore another question to gain more clarity. In each step, utilizing a model-based inquiry approach, students draw a visual of their revised mental model that explains the phenomenon or their new learning. To support her students in addressing the PBL question, Ms. Nowak developed a series of smaller learning-segment questions to guide students from the macro level of agriculture (e.g., "Why is agriculture important?") to a local issue (e.g., "How can we manage waste effectively to minimize environmental impact?"). In each learning segment, a consecutive group of daily lessons, Ms. Nowak included anchoring visuals (e.g., food supply chain and primary sources on innovations in agriculture) and sense-making activities (e.g., stories on agriculture, simulations, fertilizer experiments, and data collection on local food waste). At the end of each activity or learning segment, Ms. Nowak asked students to revise their original drawing of agriculture and its connection to society (i.e., restaurants, people). See Table 4.4 for more details.

In formatively assessing students' mastery of content, the 3D Assessment approach is utilized to assess all three dimensions of the NGSS (science and engineering practice, disciplinary core idea, and crosscutting concept). Here students are not just assessed for the content knowledge but instead asked to engage in authentic scientific thinking and practices to solve real-world problems, analyze data, and draw conclusions. Through this process, all three dimensions of the NGSS are addressed. For example, students might be provided with a new phenomenon or sample data and asked to make sense of the data and create an argument that shows their understanding. Ms. Nowak chose to have her students use technology to visualize a model eco-friendly community and then use recyclable materials to create a 3D rendering. As such, her assessment allowed students to demonstrate content knowledge and understanding of crosscutting concepts and engage in science and engineering practices (i.e., develop and use models).

In engineering and mathematics education, the curricular process is similar but often starts with a real-world problem. In both fields, the problem-based learning approach is utilized to make the content culturally relevant. Students are provided with a real-world problem and asked to use mathematics and engineering in practical application to solve the problem. In mathematics, students utilize mathematical practices along with content knowledge to provide solutions. In engineering, students engage in the engineering design process. "The engineering design process emphasizes open-ended problem solving and encourages students to learn from failure" (Teach Engineering, n.d.). In PBL and the engineering design process, the solution is open-ended and lends itself to student creativity. One of the reasons Ms. Nowak chose to design a STEAM unit is because she wanted to integrate science, engineering, and mathematics. As such, throughout her unit, students were using math to better understand implications of agriculture (e.g., calculating changes in ratio/percentage of agricultural land, calculating concentrations of fertilizer and pesticides, and creating data tables and graphs of food consumption and waste). Toward the end of the unit, as students developed their model, they engaged in engineering design to revise their model.

The Elements

To add to the above, which discusses models for the learning process, the gold standard of PBL suggests seven elements to include throughout the learning process: (1) challenging problem or question; (2) sustained inquiry; (3) authenticity; (4) student voice and choice; (5) reflection; (6) critique and revision; and (7) public product. Figure 4.3 shows the relationship between AST and PBL. First, "the project is framed by a meaningful problem to be solved or a question to answer, at the appropriate level of challenge" (i.e., challenging problem or question, PBLWorks, n.d.). PBL is often completed by groups. Through group projects situated in real life, Ms. Nowak's students engage in collective critical thinking and concurrently learn from one another as they address the problem or question. Further, PBL requires students to engage in a "rigorous, extended process of posing questions, finding resources, and applying information" (i.e., critical inquiry). Because Ms. Nowak situated the project in a real-world context and it aligned with standards and her students' interests and concerns (i.e., authenticity), her PBL curriculum design lends itself well to being culturally responsive.

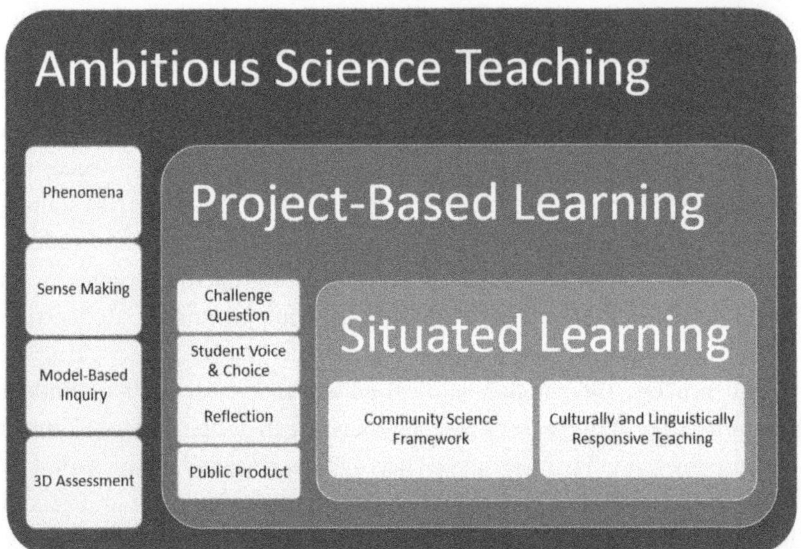

Figure 4.3 Relationship of Core Unit Elements

Throughout the unit, students led the decision process, including developing questions and determining focus, group norms, assessment product, and presentation style (i.e., student voice and choice). By including the students' voices and choices throughout the process (e.g., asking students their interests and connections, creating their own visual to show interconnectedness, sorting into groups that connect to their schema), Ms. Nowak helped her students become co-creators. Additionally, Ms. Nowak added multicultural perspectives (e.g., drawing on Angola's and Venezuela's practices and collecting data from the school) to the content to ensure that students saw themselves within the process and the content. Through the reflective process, students worked with their teacher to reflect on their inquiry, learning how they collectively overcame obstacles, thereby building and reflecting on their empathy. As Ms. Nowak's students engaged in the PBL unit, they were encouraged to "give, receive, and apply feedback to improve their process and products" (PBLWorks, n.d.). Since the product was public, Ms. Nowak's class sought feedback from community members and families along with peers and teachers so that the solution or product was authentically meeting the needs of stakeholders.

Culturally Responsive Unit Design: Situated Learning

Culturally responsive teaching situates the learning process and content in the lived experiences of students while also learning about others' lived experiences. If students do not see themselves in the unit or do not see the value or connection of the unit to themselves or the community, they are not as likely to engage with the content. To make units culturally responsive, Ms. Nowak drew on the Community Science Framework (CSF), which recommends centering community priorities (e.g., ASTC). That is, CSF suggests starting by listening to community voices and having the community play an integral part in designing the question. By doing so, the curriculum is both relevant and inclusive of students, families, and communities. Further, CSF centers community strengths in their framework by honoring the knowledge and insights of the community in the design of the project (ASTC, n.d.). CSF suggests that teachers discuss community assets and leverage diverse perspectives to support developing solutions or addressing needs. CSF is equity-focused and suggests that students, instructors, families, and community members co-construct the learning and experience (ASTC, n.d.). As such, there is shared leadership and voice. By co-creating the space, all individuals should see themselves reflected. Ms. Nowak's unit embodies CSF, as she chose a topic relevant to the community and created opportunity for community voice and input throughout—both in data collection and feedback on the model eco-friendly community that the students would produce.

As teachers, we want students not only to see themselves in the curriculum but to be able to answer the question, "When will I ever use this in real life?" The answer to this question is rooted in advocacy and agency. That is, not only can a unit be used to teach students the relevance of STEAM content, but it can teach students how to use STEAM to make actionable change within their community (i.e., social justice). Through this approach, teachers can empower students to see how they and their community have the capability to "influence science and policy-making institutions to better consider diverse community partners and democratize approaches and structures" (ASTC, n.d.). Beyond policy and structural changes, students are "creating and enacting innovative solutions to scientific and societal questions and problems" that address the priorities of the community by embedding the public product (i.e., assessment) in social action. By situating her students in the role of STEAM professionals, Ms. Nowak's unit has the "potential to expand scientific literacy and self-efficacy as well as conceptions of who can be a scientist" (i.e., increase science agency; ASTC, n.d.). That is, by developing real solutions to real-world problems, her students could redefine their role as advocates and change agents.

What Does a Culturally and Linguistically Responsive STEAM Unit Look Like?

Table 4.3 provides a unit plan template, and Table 4.4 provides an example unit storyline that Ms. Nowak designed for her students. The storyline includes the overarching question, individual learning segment questions, anchoring visuals, what students do and figure out, as well as how they represent their knowledge. The storyline is utilized to show how students engage in STEAM content and practices to better understand how they can support their own community. By developing a storyline, Ms. Nowak can be intentional in scaffolding and building student understanding of agriculture from both a local and a global context. The companion website provides a full, detailed unit storyline.

What Is the Process of Designing a Culturally and Linguistically Responsive STEAM Unit?

Unit planning is a broad, overarching process that requires centering culturally and linguistically responsive teaching. Culturally and linguistically responsive teaching should not be seen as an add-on after the unit design but an integral aspect of unit design. Considering MLs allows for intentional incorporation of ML interest, assets, and supports. Table 4.5 highlights the broad elements of unit design along with sample

Table 4.3 Unit Plan Template

Student, Family, Community Connection:			
PBL Challenge Question:			
Standards			
NGSS: **ISTE:** **NGSS (Engineering):** **NCAS:** **CCSS:** **Social Justice:** **ISBE CRTL:**			
Public Product:			
Learning Segment Questions	**Anchoring Visual**	**What We Do and Figure Out**	**How We Represent It**
Learning Segment 1 (x Periods) [Question]		What we do: What we figure out: What we do: What we figure out:	
Learning Segment 2 (x Periods) [Question]		What we do: What we figure out: What we do: What we figure out:	
Learning Segment 3 (x Periods) [Question]		What we do: What we figure out: What we do: What we figure out:	
Learning Segment 4 (x Periods) [Question]		What we do: What we figure out: What we do: What we figure out:	

Adapted from Next Generation Science Storyline (n.d.), https://www.nextgenstorylines.org/what-are-storylines

activities found in the unit storyline, the generalized language for the ML strategy associated with it, and the enacted core principles and key teaching practices in the ESEM Framework. The table demonstrates that culturally and linguistically responsive teaching is integrated throughout the unit seamlessly to support MLs.

Table 4.4 Unit Storyline Sample

Learning Segment Questions	Anchoring Visual	What We Do and Figure Out	How We Represent It
PBL Challenge Question: How can we design an eco-friendly agricultural community that meets the needs of our community while protecting the environment?			
		Learning Segment 1 (1 Period)	
Why is agriculture important?	Google Timelapse video of community	See companion website for details	KWL Visual model representing the interconnectedness of agriculture and societal elements (word bank with images provided)
		Learning Segment 2 (3 Periods)	
What/whom does agriculture impact?	Images of families, restaurants, grocery stores, animals	See companion website for details	Revised visual model to include clarity, changes, additions to relationships. We include implications. We add Post-its for questions.

Table 4.4 (*Continued*)

Learning Segment Questions	Anchoring Visual	What We Do and Figure Out	How We Represent It
		Learning Segment 3 (4 Periods)	
What/who impacts agriculture?	Images from news articles from a variety of countries as well as neighboring communities	**What we do:** We read *The Farm That Feeds Us: A Year in the Life of an Organic Farm* by Nancy Castaldo (2020). **What we figure out:** We understand agriculture in the context of seasons. We learn what happens daily on the farm, what equipment is needed, and what happens to crops during each season. **What we do:** We review our visual model to identify things that impact farming. We test out different hypotheses (e.g., temperature, fertilizer, pesticides). **What we figure out:** The role of climate change on specific crop growth. We identify concentrations of fertilizer and other additions that are most impactful. We learn about organic options, GMOs and pesticides that help crops but may negatively impact consumers and animals. We learn how climate change/temperature impacts current crops. **What we do:** We engage in the Cornucopia Virtual Simulation. **What we figure out:** We learn the role of water, land resources, weather, and climate and agricultural technologies in agriculture. **What we do:** We explore articles on the impact of pollution on crops. **What we figure out:** We figure out pollution from neighboring areas has impacts on local agriculture. **What we do:** We watch a documentary on Venezuela agricultural. **What we figure out:** There are many levels of impacts, from policy to access.	We revisit our model and add details.

Table 4.4 (*Continued*)

PBL Challenge Question: How can we design an eco-friendly agricultural community that meets the needs of our community while protecting the environment?

Learning Segment Questions	Anchoring Visual	What We Do and Figure Out	How We Represent It
		Learning Segment 4 (3 Periods)	
How can we manage waste effectively to minimize environmental impact?	Food supply chain image	See companion website for details	We add waste management details to our visual
		Learning Segment 5 (3 Periods)	
What are others doing to address agricultural concerns? (i.e., What are the best practices for sustainable agriculture?)	A series of primary sources on innovations in agriculture	See companion website for details	We add potential solutions to our visual
		Learning Segment 6 (2 Periods)	
How can we design an eco-friendly agricultural community that meets the needs of our community while protecting the environment?	Our "How We Represent It" visual	See companion website for details	Public product

Table 4.5 Sample Elements in a Unit With Culturally and Linguistically Responsive Teaching and ESEM Framework Enactment

Unit Design Component	Storyline Component	Culturally and Linguistically Responsive Teaching	Enacted ESEM Framework
Unit Focus: Ms. Nowak interviewed the students to better understand prior knowledge and experience. She drew on Angola and Venezuela assets and stories to provide global context.	**Lesson Question:** How can we design an eco-friendly agricultural community that meets the needs of our community while protecting the environment?	• Open-ended • Real-life connection • Connects to students' lives • Connects to students' cultural assets • Relevant to local community • Actionable • Aligned to WIDA standards and explicitly incorporates them throughout unit	P1.1 Ensure that curriculum content is relevant, inclusive, and accessible to all students. P1.4 Provide opportunities for MLs to see themselves reflected positively in the curriculum and learning environment.
Standards: Aligned unit to NGSS, CCSS, ISTE, NCAS, WIDA, ISBE CRTL	**What we figure out:** We learn that different countries are addressing their agricultural problems in different ways. Angola chose to change the crops they grew. Venezuela chooses to import agriculture.	• Focus on conceptual connections • Provide scaffolds to access, process and connect learning (see Chapter 5)	P1.2 Design learning units that are informed by standards and critical issues in the local and global communities.

(Continued)

Table 4.5 (*Continued*)

Unit Design Component	Storyline Component	Culturally and Linguistically Responsive Teaching	Enacted ESEM Framework
Assessment: Students work in groups to create a public product. The product will be created through the use of TinkerCad and SocraticAI. TinkerCad will be used to create a model of the product. Students will then create a physical model using recyclable material. Socratic will be used to explain the elements of the public product. Students will choose whom they would like to present to (i.e., the most relevant audience).	**How we represent it:** Visual model representing the interconnectedness of agriculture and societal elements (word bank with images provided)	• Provide multiple options for students to show what they know (i.e., assessments) • Provide scaffolds for support (e.g., word bank, sentence stems) • Create open-ended tasks/ questions • Provide paralleled outputs (e.g., visual with word) • Ask students to make connections • Involve collaboration and dialogue for meaning making	P4.1 Foster a classroom culture that respects each other, values critical thinking, and builds community. P4.3 Facilitate collaborative learning experiences that promote critical inquiry, evaluate multiple perspectives, and build empathy. P4.4 Provide opportunities for MLs to generate evidence-based arguments on social justice topics, drawing on their diverse cultural perspectives and experiences.
	Anchoring visual: Images from news articles from a variety of countries as well as neighboring communities	Decenter English as a prerequisite for conceptual understanding Choose accessible and inclusive visuals Create open-ended prompts Create opportunity to share argument	P1.5 Implement teaching strategies that recognize and value MLs' linguistic and cultural assets.
	What we do: We survey local businesses, our school, and our family to track food consumption and waste. We graph our results and present the data as fractions/ratios and percentages. We compare it to the national average.	Include a variety of activities/ inputs, such as fictional reading, videos, articles, visual analysis, primary sources, data, technology simulations, hands-on inquiry Provide translations when available	P4.2 Encourage MLs to critically examine issues of power, privilege, and inequality in a disciplinary context.

Conclusion

This chapter has outlined the essential elements of STEAM unit design and assessment. By leveraging the project-based learning model in conjunction with best math and science practices (e.g., Ambitious Science Teaching, PBL, and Community Science Framework), teachers are able to make learning accessible, engaging, relevant, and asset-based for all students, including MLs. Storylines support students in making connections throughout the unit while also allowing them to track their understanding toward the culminating project. By framing the unit around an actionable project, students are positioned to use STEAM content as they advocate for their community.

The chapter is built around the belief that curriculum design should not use an additive approach when considering MLs but instead center student experiences, knowledge, and assets. In doing so, MLs can see themselves throughout the unit and have multiple entry points as well as ways to show what they know. The companion website provides additional resources related to the topics in this chapter. The next chapter discusses how to design STEAM instruction with differentiation and support strategies for MLs in day-to-day lessons.

References

Ambitious Science Teaching. (n.d.). *Get started.* https://ambitiousscienceteaching.org/get-started/

Association of Science and Technology Centers (ASTC). (n.d.). *Community science framework.* https://communityscience.astc.org/framework/

Castaldo, N. (2020). *The farm that feeds us: A year in the life of an organic farm.* QUarto.

Council of Chief State School Officers. (2010). *Common core state standards for mathematics.* http://www.corestandards.org/Math/

International Society for Technology in Education. (2016). *ISTE standards for students.* https://www.iste.org/standards/for-students

National Coalition for Core Arts Standards. (2014). *National core arts standards.* https://www.nationalartsstandards.org/

Next Generation Science Standards. (n.d.a). *Next generation science standards.* https://www.nextgenscience.org/

Next Generation Science Standards. (n.d.b). *Assessment resources.* https://www.nextgenscience.org/assessment-resources/assessment-resources

Next Generation Science Storylines. (n.d.). *What are storylines?* https://www.nextgenstorylines.org/what-are-storylines

PBLWorks. (n.d.). *Gold standard project-based learning: Essential project design elements.* https://www.pblworks.org/what-is-pbl/gold-standard

Teach Engineering. (n.d.). *Engineering design process.* https://www.teachengineering.org/populartopics/designprocess

Wiggins, G., & McTighe, J. (2012) *The understanding by design guide to creating high-quality units.* Association for Supervision and Curriculum Development.

5

STEAM Instruction and Linguistic Justice

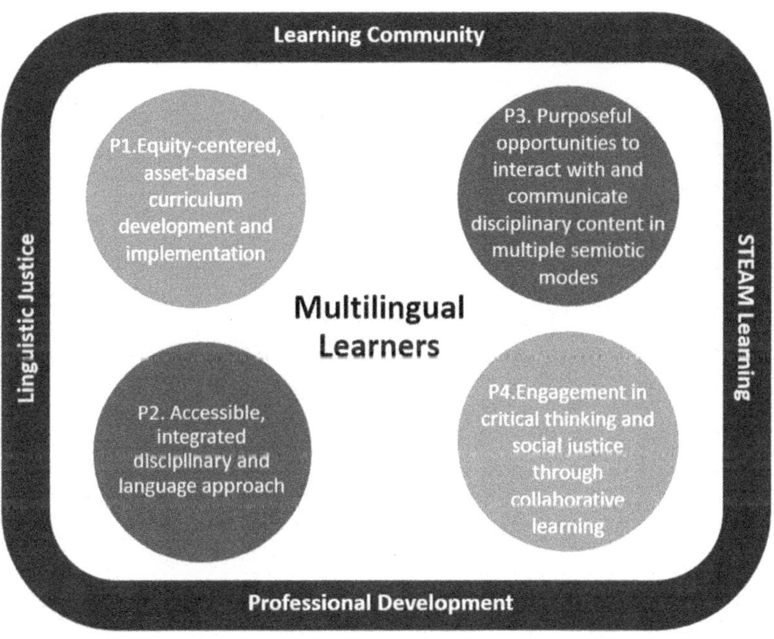

Figure 5.1 ESEM Framework

In this chapter, we shift the focus from the broader aspects of STEAM curriculum planning, implementation, and assessment to examine the dynamics of daily STEAM instruction and how educators can bring linguistic justice to STEAM learning. Anchored in the ESEM Framework, the chapter draws on Class Profile 2 (see Table 5.2) to demonstrate

Table 5.1 Focused Core Principles and Key Practices in ESEM Framework

Focused Core Principles	Key Teaching Practices
P2. Accessible, integrated disciplinary and language approach	P2.1 Provide explicit instruction on how languages and culture work for disciplines. P2.2 Scaffold language use in disciplinary contexts, supporting MLs' comprehension and expression throughout investigations. P2.3 Facilitate repeated exposure to and practice of language within meaningful disciplinary contexts. P2.4 Provide opportunities for MLs to engage in disciplinary practices (such as scientific inquiry and mathematical problem-solving) by using their language skills. P2.5 Promote translanguaging as a valid language practice that supports MLs' learning across disciplines.
P3. Purposeful opportunities to interact with and communicate disciplinary content in multiple semiotic modes	P3.1 Design interactive learning experiences that immerse MLs in a diverse range of semiotic modes. P3.2 Provide differentiated multimodal disciplinary content adaptive to MLs' learning preferences and linguistic needs. P3.3 Integrate technology tools and sense-making resources that support MLs' engagement with disciplinary content. P3.4 Scaffold MLs' use of multiple semiotic modes to express their understanding of disciplinary concepts and communicate their ideas effectively. P3.5 Encourage MLs to create and share multimodal projects that demonstrate their understanding of disciplinary concepts and skills and enhanced proficiency in multiple languages.

how to design effective instruction and implement differentiation ideas and strategies that foster MLs' meaningful STEAM learning. Chapter 5 resources on the publisher's companion website provide additional information related to the topics discussed in this chapter.

Mr. Gilbert made Earth Day special for his students by introducing them to the environmental issue of oil spills through the picture book

Table 5.2 Class Profile 2

Context	Suburban, 3rd grade, ESL pull-out and push-in model
Teachers	**Mr. Gilbert** (a monolingual English classroom teacher) and **Ms. Fang** (a bilingual Chinese/English ESL teacher)

Selected ML Profiles	**Olha**
	• Born in Ukraine but moved with her family to the US six months ago. Olha is considered a newcomer.
	• **Ukrainian**
	  ○ Oracy: expanding
	  ○ Literacy: developing
	• **English**
	  ○ Oracy: emerging
	  ○ Literacy: entering
	
	Lin
	• Born in Australia to Chinese parents and moved back to China when he was five years old. The family immigrated to the US one year ago.
	• **Chinese**
	  ○ Oracy: developing
	  ○ Literacy: beginning
	• **English**
	  ○ Oracy: developing
	  ○ Literacy: emerging

Black Beach: A Community, an Oil Spill, and the Origin of Earth Day by Shaunna Stith and John Stith (2023). The story sparked curiosity and compassion as students learned how communities, like the one in which the school is located, can unite to protect the environment. Following the reading, Mr. Gilbert engaged the students in exploring how oil spills occur, their impact on marine life, and how science and technology can be used for cleanup efforts, including the use of magnets to remove oil from water. To make the lesson interactive, Mr. Gilbert organized a hands-on activity where students simulated an oil spill and experimented with different cleanup methods, including using magnets and iron filings. These instructional activities connected their Earth Day celebration to real-world environmental science and engineering, sparking excitement and reflection on how students can contribute to protecting the Earth.

How to Design Effective STEAM Instruction?

Designing effective STEAM instruction involves several approaches that align with the core principles in the ESEM Framework, particularly P2: Accessible, integrated disciplinary and language approach; and P3: Purposeful opportunities to interact with and communicate disciplinary content in multiple semiotic modes (see details in Table 5.1). First, community-based inquiry projects offer students opportunities to connect their learning to local issues and organizations, fostering a sense of civic responsibility and environmental stewardship. For example, students can collaborate with local environmental organizations to study water quality in nearby rivers or lakes, using scientific tools to analyze their findings and propose solutions. Another project might involve partnering with local businesses to design eco-friendly packaging, allowing students to apply principles of engineering, sustainability, and design in a practical setting. Chapter 6 focuses on partnerships with families and communities, where we introduce more ideas for community-focused projects that provide real-world relevance and prepare students for future career possibilities.

Visual literacy, along with critical visual literacy, is another key component of STEAM education and is applied in three primary ways. First, there are many existing visual data sets in STEAM, such as maps, diagrams, data tables, and graphs, that require students to interpret and analyze patterns and meaning (Moline, 2021). Further, students can actively develop data collection tools, such as surveys and interviews, and gather data from their everyday experiences. For instance, students might conduct a survey of their school's energy usage. They could then present the data in a visual format for analysis.

Second, critical visual literacy goes beyond interpreting and analyzing visuals to examining the power relations embedded in sociocultural contexts (Chung, 2013). Students are encouraged to ask critical questions, such as: Who created this visual, and who is the intended audience? Why was this visual created? Why were the data presented this way? Who is represented, and who is missing? Who benefits from it? For example, students could examine the map of notorious oil spills around the world (https://amazonfrontlines.org/chronicles/health-oil/) and explore why the most notorious oil spills took place in the northern Ecuadorian Amazon and which communities became the victims of countless spills.

By asking these questions, students can develop critical consciousness of power hierarchy and activate their agency to propose solutions for change toward equity and social justice. For example, after learning about the impact of oil spills on the environment and communities, students might investigate ways to mitigate such damage in their own community. They could develop proposals to raise awareness about oil dependency, advocate for cleaner energy sources, or design prototypes of oil spill containment solutions, like absorbent barriers or eco-friendly materials that help prevent the spread of oil.

Third, visual literacy includes the use of visual tools to support and deepen content understanding. Tools such as graphic organizers (e.g., flowcharts, Venn diagrams, cause-and-effect charts, and concept maps) provide a visual framework for organizing and connecting complex ideas, helping both teachers and students understand the relationships between key concepts. For teachers, these tools guide lesson planning by linking standards with hands-on activities, such as connecting oil spills to broader environmental and engineering principles. For example, Figure 5.2 illustrates the integration of NGSS and ML supports in an oil spill unit. At the center is the topic "Oil Spills," connected to various educational components. The NGSS aspects include the science and engineering practices (SEP), disciplinary core ideas (DCI), and crosscutting concepts (XCC). Under SEP, students are encouraged to engage in asking questions and defining problems. DCI focuses on concepts such as the interaction between magnets and the human impact of environmental disasters, tied to standard 3-PS2-4. XCC emphasizes the historical and cultural context of magnetism, including maglev trains in China and cow magnets in Ukraine, bridging scientific principles with engineering solutions. Meanwhile, ML supports help develop instruction that takes into consideration students' language proficiency levels, activates or builds background knowledge and prior experience, and provides focused differentiation and strategies to support MLs' language and content development.

For students, visual tools help in breaking down abstract concepts into manageable components, fostering deeper comprehension through clear connections between science, technology, mathematics, and real-world issues. Additionally, visual tools scaffold learning for MLs by providing structured pathways to develop both content and language.

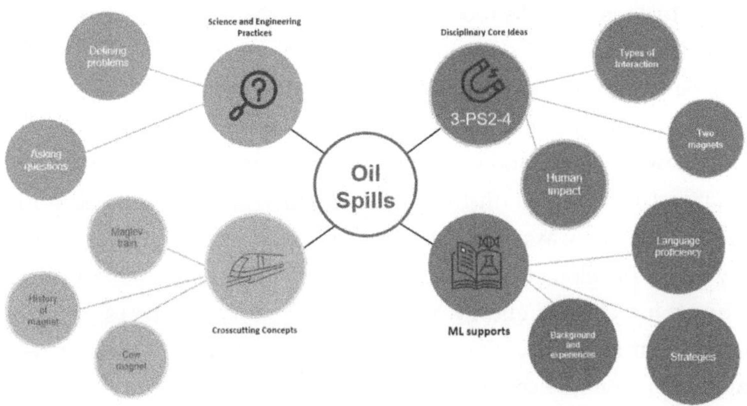

Figure 5.2 Concept Map of Oil Spills Unit: Integrating NGSS and ML Support

Key questions, particularly those that are student generated and aligned with NGSS standards, play a central role in STEAM classrooms. By encouraging students to ask open-ended and Socratic questions, teachers foster critical thinking and inquiry. For instance, asking the question, "How can we design a water filtration system using only natural materials?," allows students to explore engineering and scientific principles while developing problem-solving skills. These types of student-centered questions deepen understanding and promote connections across STEAM disciplines.

Further, a series of sense-making activities are essential in each lesson, with multiple activities often incorporated to help students process and synthesize their learning. For example, students may brainstorm solutions, engage in hands-on experiments, and reflect on their findings through group discussions or presentations. This iterative process supports students in making meaningful connections between different STEAM concepts.

Finally, performance-based and differentiated assessments are key to evaluating student learning. These assessments allow students to demonstrate their understanding through creative projects, presentations, and real-world applications rather than traditional tests. Differentiated assessment strategies ensure that all students, regardless of their learning styles or abilities, can show what they know and connect their learning to real-world challenges.

By integrating community-based inquiry, visual literacy and critical visual literacy, student-centered questioning, sense-making activities, and performance-based assessments, educators are able to design dynamic and engaging STEAM instruction. These strategies not only foster critical thinking and problem-solving, but also connect students' learning to real-world issues, empowering them to apply their STEAM knowledge in meaningful and impactful ways. In the next section, we will address how STEAM educators bring linguistic justice to STEAM classrooms with MLs.

How to Bring Linguistic Justice to STEAM Learning?

WIDA ELD Framework and Can-Do Descriptors

To elaborate more on the Core Principle 2, we will first revisit the WIDA (2020) English Language Development (ELD) framework and Can-Do Descriptors introduced in Chapter 1. WIDA (2016) further breaks down the Can-Do Descriptors by each of the four language domains based on the four key language uses: narrate, inform, explain, and argue. The last two key language uses—explain and argue—are the most prominent in the STEAM context. Table 5.3 provides examples of what Olha and Lin can achieve by the end of their specific proficiency levels in performing the key language use of *explain* in English.

Expanding language expectations from the four language domains—listening, speaking, reading, and writing—to two broader modes of communication—interpretive and expressive—not only increases accessibility for MLs by moving beyond just oral and written language but also emphasizes the multimodal nature of communication (WIDA, 2020). An important note is that MLs often fall in varying proficiency levels across different modes of communication. Some MLs may demonstrate higher proficiency in interpretive modes like listening, reading, and viewing, while others may excel in expressive modes such as speaking, writing, and representing. This variability across communication modes, as well as differences among various languages or language varieties, highlights the

Table 5.3 Can-Do Descriptors in Language Domains, Key Language Use of Explain

Key Language Use of *Explain*			
Students	Language Domains		
	Listening	Speaking	Reading	Writing
Olha	*Emerging* Process explanations by • Matching oral descriptions to photos, pictures, or icons • Following simple sequences presented orally to create patterns or sequences	*Emerging* Explain by • Naming steps in processes or procedures • Describing familiar phenomena in words or phrases	*Entering* Process explanations by • Identifying words and phrases in titles and highlighted texts • Matching pictures with graphic information from illustrated texts	*Entering* Explain by • Listing and illustrating ideas • Stating facts associated with images or illustrations
Lin	*Developing* Process explanations by • Carrying out steps described orally to solve problems • Completing graphic organizers or representations from oral comparisons	*Developing* Explain by • Describing relationships between objects or uses for tools • Expressing cause and effect of behaviors or events	*Emerging* Process explanations by • Interpreting images, illustrations, and graphics • Identifying elements of expository texts (e.g., graphs, captions) in illustrated texts	*Emerging* Explain by • Describing elements of processes or procedures • Stating how something happens using illustrations and sequential language (e.g., eruption of volcanoes)

Adapted from WIDA (2016), https://wida.wisc.edu/teach/can-do/descriptors

dynamic nature of language learning, which is influenced by sociocultural factors such as the context in which language is used, the topic, the audience, and the purpose for communication. This understanding emphasizes the importance for teachers to possess the knowledge and skills to effectively design and implement differentiated instruction so that MLs receive appropriate scaffolding tailored to their unique language needs. Such an approach is essential for helping MLs meet language expectations while demonstrating their subject area knowledge and skills.

Linguistic Justice: Differentiation and Strategies

Linguistic justice is one of the four walls on the ESEM Framework. It is addressed in two ways in this chapter: differentiation and strategies. We first explain how to differentiate instructions for MLs, as differentiation is a broader approach with the purpose of adapting instruction based on learners' individual needs. This is followed by a discussion on strategies, which are specific tools that teachers can use to provide language support for MLs while they learn the disciplinary content.

Differentiating instruction at the elementary level can be approached through content, process, product, and affect (Tomlinson & Imbeau, 2010). To differentiate content, for instance, teachers can provide the text in English and MLs' primary language, or at different reading levels for different students. In addition to these general differentiation strategies, how would teachers go about differentiating instruction for MLs? Fairbairn and Jones-Vo (2010) provide specific guidance that supports teachers to accomplish this challenge (see Table 5.4).

The differentiation template starts with content objectives that are aligned with the standards. Although MLs are at different language

Table 5.4 Differentiation Template for MLs

Content Objective
ML Name & Language Proficiency Levels
English & Translanguaging Objectives
Differentiated Support

Adapted from Fairbairn & Jones-Vo (2010)

proficiency levels, it is a priority to hold high expectations for all students and use the same standards-based content objectives. For this reason, the first row of the differentiation template in Table 5.4 is bolded to suggest that the information should be the same for all students. Followed by the content objectives are MLs' language proficiency levels, language objectives, and differentiated support. These three rows are not bolded because the information will be different for each ML. For example, in row two, every ML's language proficiency level may vary. In the third row, the English and translanguaging objectives would differ based on what each ML can do at their specific proficiency level. The fourth and final row indicates differentiated support needed for MLs to meet both content and language objectives. The last two rows are where teachers can refer to the WIDA (2016) Can-Do Descriptors for key language use, content stem, and support.

Further, differentiation for MLs is not solely the responsibility of language specialists like ESL teachers but should involve all educators (WIDA, 2012a, 2012b). In the second part of this chapter, we will present specific examples of how Mr. Gilbert and Ms. Fang differentiated instruction for Olha and Lin within the context of STEAM activities.

The ML strategies we propose are grounded in a functional perspective on language (Halliday, 1975), translanguaging pedagogy (García et al., 2016), and multimodal communication (NASEM, 2018; WIDA, 2020)—all of which were introduced and explained in the first two chapters of the book. The contemporary focus on language development has shifted toward "language for disciplinary areas," as outlined in the WIDA (2020) framework. In other words, discipline-specific vocabulary and terminology are no longer seen as prerequisites for accessing STEAM content. Instead, language is viewed as a tool for engaging in STEAM practices. A similar shift has occurred in STEAM education, with a growing emphasis on "knowledge-in-use" (Lee & Stephens, 2020), rather than simply mastering a set of content knowledge and skills.

Informed by the latest research on language development and STEAM education, we present a list of ML strategies in Table 5.5 that are aligned with the ESEM framework. The strategies are organized based on the stages and language domains involved in a STEAM activity. While not exhaustive, these strategies provide a starting point for incorporating asset-based, language-as-function, translanguaging, and multimodal perspectives into daily instruction.

Table 5.5 ML Strategies in STEAM Instruction

Before Instruction	During Instruction	
	Interpretive Mode: *Listening, Reading, and Viewing*	**Expressive Mode:** *Speaking, Writing, and Representing*
• Research and assess MLs' background knowledge on topic • Invite MLs to share language and home/cultural practices connected to the activity • Activate or build background knowledge on topic if necessary	• Provide instruction, materials, resources, and learning experiences at appropriate levels, in different languages, or in different modalities • Facilitate repeated exposure to language within meaningful STEAM context • Scaffold language use in STEAM contexts, supporting MLs' comprehension throughout investigations • Support MLs in developing metalinguistic awareness • Flexible grouping	• Create space for MLs to leverage all linguistic and cultural resources and multiple modalities • Facilitate repeated practice of language within meaningful STEAM context • Support MLs in bridging language use from diverse, informal registers to the formal registers used by STEM professionals • Support MLs in applying metalinguistic awareness in their own creation • Flexible grouping

What Does STEAM Instruction With Linguistic Justice Look Like in the Classroom?

We will present the overview of the unit plan to provide the context before we elaborate on what STEAM instruction with linguistic justice looks like. Table 5.6 outlines the unit storyline in Mr. Gilbert's classroom with sample lessons and a series of sense-making activities, discussing various ways science and engineering could be used to clean up an oil spill and protect the environment. The rationale of the unit is not only to help students connect personally to the topic but also to provide a global perspective that can enrich scientific exploration and environmental stewardship.

Within the context of the unit, we use the differentiation template provided in the chapter to develop differentiated support for Olha and Lin, focusing on the oil spill cleanup simulation. As shown in Table 5.7, the

Table 5.6 Overview of Unit Storyline

Unit Essential Question: How can we use science and engineering to clean up oil spills and protect the environment?			
Lesson Questions	**Phenomenon**	**What We Do and Figure Out**	**How We Represent It**
Lesson 1 (1 Period) What causes oil spills, and how do they harm ocean life and the environment?	Anchoring phenomenon	**What we do:** Analyze two photos related to oil spills. • **Photo of a bird stuck in an oil spill:** This image sparks curiosity about how oil spills affect wildlife and the environment. • **World map of oil spill locations:** This provides a global perspective, showing where oil spills occur and their impact on ecosystems. **What we figure out:** We have a lot of questions about the cause of oil spills and different ideas about how to clean up the oil spills and protect wildlife.	**Group Discussion:** Create a model to explain the causes of oil spills and how they impact the ecosystem.
Lesson 2 (3 Periods) What happens to water, animals, and humans when oil spills into the ocean? Can we clean up all the oil?	Photos of bird trapped in an oil spill	**What we do:** Sample Activity 1—Oil Spill Cleanup Simulation We read an article about oil spills around the world. We simulate an oil spill by pouring water and oil into containers. Add feathers, toy fish, and a rubber duck to represent animals affected by the spill. Students use sponges, cotton balls, and paper towels to try cleaning the oil. **What we figure out:** Sponges and towels absorb some oil but are not completely effective. Magnets can pull the iron filings (and attached oil) out of the water, making them a faster cleanup tool. Discuss the key science question: How do magnets help clean up oil spills?	**Group Discussion:** Share observations of the different cleanup methods. **Presentation:** Students explain which cleanup method they think is best and why.

Table 5.6 (*Continued*)

Unit Essential Question: How can we use science and engineering to clean up oil spills and protect the environment?			
Lesson Questions	**Phenomenon**	**What We Do and Figure Out**	**How We Represent It**
Lesson 3 (3 Periods) How much oil did we clean up with sponges? How much faster was the magnet compared to other tools?	Measuring cylinders, digital balance and a stopwatch	**What we do:** Sample Activity 2—Measuring Oil Cleanup We estimate and measure the amount of oil cleaned from the water using sponges and magnets. We create a graph to show the amount of oil cleaned using different methods. **What we figure out:** We represent the amount of oil cleaned as a fraction of the total oil (e.g., "We cleaned ¼ of the oil with sponges."). We time how long it takes to clean the oil with magnets versus sponges and compare the results.	**Graph:** Students create a group graph showing the results of their experiment. **Group Discussion:** Students use math to compare which method worked faster.
Lesson 4 (2 Periods) How can we design a device to prevent two moving objects from touching each other?	Photos of examples of magnets in everyday life (compass, magnetic clasps on jewelry, magnet toys, speakers, etc.)	**What we do:** Sample Activity 3—Engineering Challenge We use magnets, string, and craft materials to design and construct a latch that keeps a door shut. We design a device that prevents two moving toy cars from colliding, using magnets or other barriers. **What we figure out:** Magnets can hold doors shut by attracting the latch to a metal surface, and they can push objects apart, keeping them from touching.	**Group Presentations:** Students demonstrate how their latch or device works and explain their design choices.

(*Continued*)

Table 5.6 (*Continued*)

Unit Essential Question: How can we use science and engineering to clean up oil spills and protect the environment?			
Lesson Questions	**Phenomenon**	**What We Do and Figure Out**	**How We Represent It**
Lesson 5 (2 Periods) How do maglev trains use magnets to move faster? What does it mean when magnets attract or repel each other?	Video clips of maglev trains	**What we do:** Sample Activity 4—Exploring Magnetism We watch a video about maglev trains and discuss how magnets help the trains float above the tracks. Students explore how magnets can make a toy car move without touching it. Students use iron filings and magnets to create art that visualizes magnetic fields. **What we figure out:** Magnets repel or attract depending on their poles. Maglev trains reduce friction by floating above the tracks using magnetic force.	**Magnet Art Display:** Students display and explain their magnetic field artwork. **Group Discussion:** Students explain how magnets help maglev trains move quickly.
Lesson 6 (1 Period) How have magnets been used historically and in modern times to solve problems around the world?	Maps of China and Ukraine Images of ancient compasses, maglev trains, and cow magnets	**What we do:** Sample Activity 5—Cultural Connections We look at a map of China and discuss the historical discovery of magnets over 2,000 years ago. We learn about how ancient sailors used magnets in the compass to navigate the seas. We examine a map of Ukraine and learn how magnets are used in agriculture. Farmers use cow magnets to protect cows from swallowing harmful metal objects while grazing. **What we figure out:** We figure out that magnets were essential in navigation and exploration, helping people travel safely using the compass. We also understand that magnets are now used in advanced technology like maglev trains, where they help reduce friction and make transportation faster and more efficient.	**Group discussion:** Create a class chart to organize these examples and connect them to the real-world applications of magnets, such as cleaning up oil spills.

Table 5.7 Differentiation for MLs in the Third-Grade Classroom

Content Objective	Students will be able to describe the different methods that environmental engineers use to clean up oil spills.	

ML Name & Language Proficiency Levels	**Olha**
	• **Ukrainian**
	  ◦ Oracy: expanding
	  ◦ Literacy: developing
	• **English**
	  ◦ Oracy: emerging
	  ◦ Literacy: entering
		Lin
		• **Chinese**
		  ◦ Oracy: developing
		  ◦ Literacy: beginning
		• **English**
		  ◦ Oracy: developing
		  ◦ Literacy: emerging

English & Translanguaging Objectives	• Orally share different oil spill cleanup methods using descriptive words and phrases in English or Ukrainian, body language, real objects, and pictures • Use simple sentences with descriptive language, occasional academic content-related vocabulary, drawing, labels, and other media • Identify scientific terms that are similar in English and Ukrainian (e.g., for the word *magnet* is *mahnit* in Ukrainian)	• Orally share different oil spill cleanup methods using simple sentences in English or Chinese, body language, real objects, and pictures • Produce descriptive words or phrases, drawing, labels, and other media • Compare and contrast the basic sentence structure between Chinese and English
Differentiated Support	• Bilingual vocabulary list • Visuals of oil spills (e.g., photos, maps, and data charts) • Experiences gained from the simulations • Picture-supported oil spill cleanup texts in Ukrainian • A think-aloud demonstration of sentence writing • A visual guide and key vocabulary for oral description • Sentence stems with a word bank to support writing and show content understanding	• Illustrated bilingual vocabulary list • Visuals of oil spills (e.g., photos, maps, and data charts) • Experiences gained from the simulations • Oil spill cleanup multimedia in English with Chinese caption • A mini lesson that compares sentence structure in English and Chinese with Ms. Fang • A visual guide with sample sentences for oral description • Tools (e.g., pencils, crayons, stickers) that support the creation of a multimedia presentation to show content understanding

content objective remains the same for all students. However, since MLs like Olha and Lin are at different proficiency levels in both English and their primary languages, we create distinct English and translanguaging objectives, offering differentiated support that builds on their strengths and promotes continuous development.

With the help of Ms. Fang, the ESL teacher who provides push-in and pull-out services for MLs, Mr. Gilbert finished drafting the differentiated support for Olha and Lin. They proceeded to integrate general ML strategies into the instruction. Table 5.8 presents sample activities in a lesson in the unit, highlighting how Mr. Gilbert and Ms. Fang incorporated various ML strategies to enact the core principles and key teaching practices in the ESEM Framework.

Figure 5.3 Turtle Rescue and Rehabilitation

NOAA's National Ocean Service. (2010). *Turtle rescue and rehabilitation.* https://commons.wikimedia.org/wiki/File:Turtle_Rescue_and_Rehabilitation.jpg

Table 5.8 Sample Activities in a Lesson with ML Strategies and ESEM Framework Enactment

Sample Activities	ML Strategies	Enacted Sample Core Principles and Key Teaching Practices
Opening: Students view the photo in Figure 5.3 and are prompted with visual thinking questions: What's going on in this picture? What do you see that makes you say that? What more can we find? Upon finishing the discussion, Mr. Gilbert provides the key questions of the lesson: What happens to water and animals when oil spills into the ocean? How can we clean up all the oil? Students brainstorm how they think oil spills might affect marine life. Use the photo to guide conversation, highlighting the challenges of cleaning up oil and protecting animals.	• Providing MLs with an accessible visual to engage in the anchoring phenomenon (Figure 5.3) • Adapted visual thinking strategy graphic organizer with visual cues and sentence stems (e.g., I see… I think… I wonder…) for MLs • Key questions are translated to MLs' primary languages • A visual word wall featuring key academic concepts/terms • Allow MLs to respond to discussion prompts using all linguistic and nonlinguistic resources	P2.2 Scaffold language use in disciplinary contexts, supporting MLs' comprehension and expression throughout investigations. P2.4 Provide opportunities for MLs to engage in disciplinary practices by using their languages in different domains. P2.5 Promote translanguaging as a valid language practice that supports MLs' learning across disciplines. P3.1 Design interactive learning experiences that immerse MLs in a diverse range of semiotic modes.

(Continued)

Table 5.8 *(Continued)*

Sample Activities	ML Strategies	Enacted Sample Core Principles and Key Teaching Practices
Oil Spill Cleanup Simulation: With a simulated oil spill (a bucket filled with oil-covered water and features representing marine life), students make predictions on which of the given materials (sponges, cotton balls, and paper towels) works the best for cleaning up the oil and why. Have students experiment by trying each material and recording how well it removes the oil from the water and feathers. Provide each group with an ice cube tray divided into 10 equal sections, representing the total amount of oil spilled, along with a worksheet that shows a similar 10-section tray diagram. Fill the tray with water and oil to simulate an oil spill. Instruct the students to clean up using the oil sponges, cotton balls, and paper towels. After completing the cleanup activity, students will color in the sections of the worksheet that correspond to the amount of oil they successfully removed. For example, if they clean oil from 3 out of the 10 sections from the ice tray, they will color in 3 sections on the worksheet and write the fraction 3/10 next to it. This will visually represent their progress in the oil cleanup. See Figure 5.4 for an example.	• Talk moves (i.e., dialogue prompts) for MLs to engage in small group collaboration • Assign ML roles that build on their academic and linguistic strengths; for example, Lin, who has stronger oracy skills than literacy skills, will take the role of the reporter, conducting a second check on the recorder's fraction calculation and practicing how to communicate the result in a complete sentence to the group	P2.3 Facilitate repeated exposure to and practice of language within meaningful disciplinary contexts. P2.4 Provide opportunities for MLs to engage in disciplinary practices (such as scientific inquiry and mathematical problem-solving) by using their languages in different domains. P3.1 Design interactive learning experiences that immerse MLs in a diverse range of semiotic modes.

Table 5.8 (*Continued*)

Sample Activities	ML Strategies	Enacted Sample Core Principles and Key Teaching Practices
Whole-Class Discussion: Bring the class together to discuss their findings. Ask questions: Which material is the most effective? How did you know? Have students use the recorded fractions as evidence to support their claim. Note how the fractions vary between groups and how different cleanup methods affected their results. Discuss: Could you clean up all the oil, or was some left behind? What other challenges did you face when cleaning the feathers? What are ways to solve these challenges? Explain that scientists and engineers are constantly exploring new ways to solve environmental problems, including using magnets to clean oil spills.	• Use the CER anchor chart with visuals and sentence stems to support MLs' STEAM discourse development • Encourage students to use all linguistic and nonlinguistic resources to communicate meaning (e.g., MLs can point to the material or use their primary language to show the most effective material if they don't know the corresponding vocabulary in English; they can also use drawings or symbols to show the challenges or possible solutions) • Activate MLs' background knowledge about the magnet application in their home countries (e.g., Lin can share about his own experience taking the maglev train in China, and Ohla, who grew up in the rural area of Ukraine, can explain how cow magnets are used)	P2.3 Facilitate repeated exposure to and practice of language within meaningful disciplinary contexts. P2.5 Promote translanguaging as a valid language practice that supports MLs' learning across disciplines. P3.4 Scaffold MLs' use of multiple semiotic modes to express their understanding of disciplinary concepts and communicate their ideas effectively.

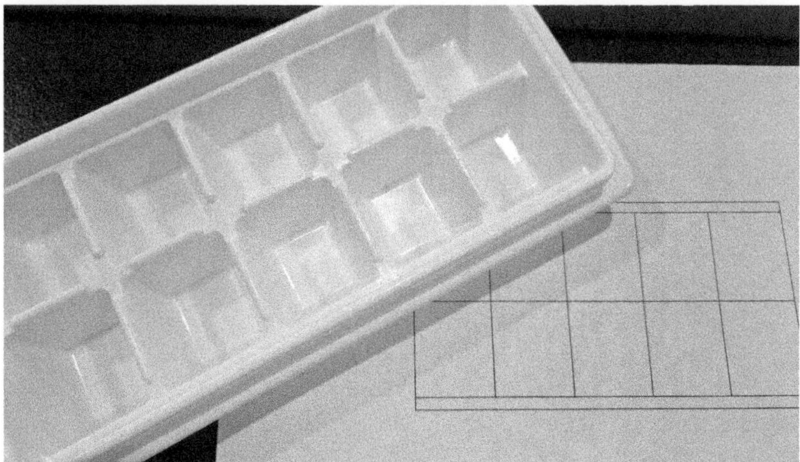

Figure 5.4 Ice Tray Activity

Conclusion

This chapter has outlined the approaches to design and implement STEAM instruction with linguistic justice. By leveraging an asset-based perspective, translanguaging pedagogy, multimodal learning strategies, and WIDA resources, educators are better equipped to provide meaningful, differentiated instruction that meets the diverse needs of MLs. Through carefully designed inquiry projects and real-world applications, such as oil spill cleanups and magnetism, students are encouraged to develop critical thinking skills, engage in scientific practices, and connect their learning to their cultural backgrounds.

The chapter emphasizes that effective STEAM instruction goes beyond content delivery; it involves creating opportunities for MLs to actively participate in scientific inquiry, engineering design, and problem-solving while utilizing their linguistic, nonlinguistic, and cultural resources. By incorporating approaches like critical visual literacy, collaborative sense-making, and performance-based assessments, educators foster an inclusive learning environment where all students can thrive. As we look ahead, the integration of these approaches and linguistic justice will continue to play a crucial role in empowering students to apply their knowledge in meaningful ways, preparing them for the challenges and opportunities of the future.

References

Chung, S. K. (2013). Critical visual literacy. *International Journal of Arts Education, 11*(2), 1–21.

Fairbairn, S., & Jones-Vo, S. (2010). *Differentiating instruction and assessment for English language learners: A guide for K-12 teachers.* Caslon.

García, O., Johnson, S., & Seltzer, K. (2016). *The translanguaging classroom: Leveraging student bilingualism for learning.* Caslon.

Halliday, M. A. K. (1975). *Learning how to mean: Explorations in the development of language.* Edward Arnold. http://dx.doi.org/10.1016/b978-0-12-443701-2.50025-1

Lee, O., & Stephens, A. (2020). English learners in STEM subjects: Contemporary views on STEM subjects and language with English learners. *Educational Researcher, 49*(6), 426–432. DOI:10.3102/0013189X20923708

Moline, S. (2021). *I see what you mean: Visual literacy K-8* (2nd ed.). Routledge.

National Academies of Sciences, Engineering, and Medicine (NASEM). (2018). *English learners in STEM subjects: Transforming classrooms, schools, and lives.* National Academies Press.

NOAA's National Ocean Service. (2010). *Turtle rescue and rehabilitation.* https://commons.wikimedia.org/wiki/File:Turtle_Rescue_and_Rehabilitation.jpg

Stith, S., & Stith, J. (2023). *Black beach: A community, an oil spill, and the origin of Earth Day.* Little Bee Books.

Tomlinson, C. A., & Imbeau, M. B. (2010). *Leading and managing a differentiated classroom.* ASCD.

WIDA. (2012a). *Focus on differentiation. Part 1.* https://edu.wyoming.gov/wp-content/uploads/2020/09/FocusOn-Differentiation-Part1.pdf

WIDA. (2012b). *Focus on differentiation. Part 2.* https://edu.wyoming.gov/wp-content/uploads/2020/09/FocusOn-Differentiation-Part2.pdf

WIDA. (2016). *Can do descriptors: Key uses edition.* https://wida.wisc.edu/sites/default/files/resource/CanDo-KeyUses-Gr-2-3.pdf

WIDA. (2020). *English Language Development (ELD) Standards Framework, 2020 edition: Kindergarten-grade 12.* Board of the University of Wisconsin System. https://wida.wisc.edu/teach/standards/eld

6

Partnership with Families and Communities with a STEAM Focus

Xiaoli Wen

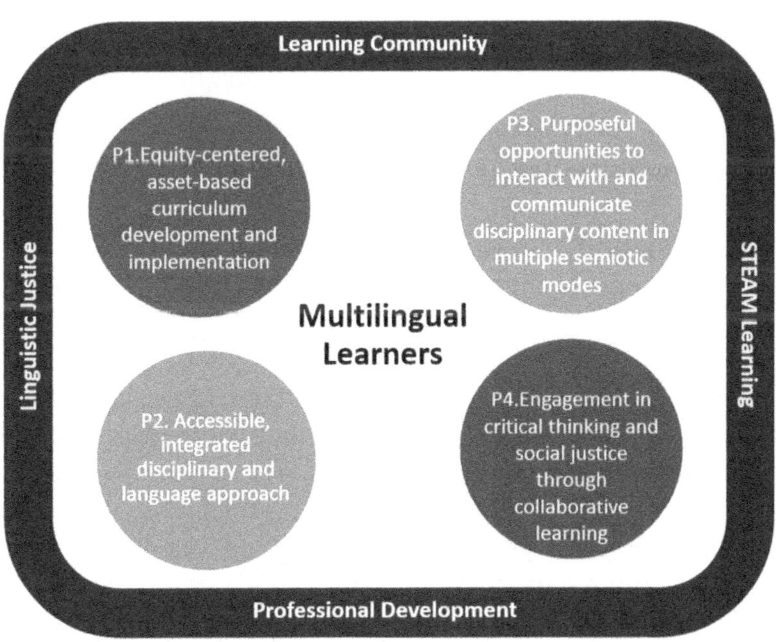

Figure 6.1 ESEM Framework

Table 6.1 Focused Core Principles and Key Teaching Practices in the ESEM Framework

Focused Core Principles	Key Teaching Practices
P1. Equity-centered, asset-based curriculum development and implementation	P1.1 Ensure that curriculum content is relevant, inclusive, and accessible to all students. P1.2 Design learning units that are informed by standards and critical issues in the local and global communities. P1.3 Develop learning experiences that reflect and build on the cultural and linguistic assets of MLs and diverse disciplinary practices. P1.4 Provide opportunities for MLs to see themselves reflected positively in the curriculum and learning environment. P1.5 Implement teaching strategies that recognize and value MLs' linguistic and cultural assets.
P4. Engagement in critical thinking and social justice through collaborative learning	P4.1 Foster a classroom culture that respects each other, values critical thinking, and builds community. P4.2 Encourage MLs to critically examine issues of power, privilege, and inequality in a disciplinary context. P4.3 Facilitate collaborative learning experiences that promote critical inquiry, evaluate multiple perspectives, and build empathy. P4.4 Provide opportunities for MLs to generate evidence-based arguments on social justice topics, drawing on their diverse cultural perspectives and experiences. P4.5 Encourage MLs to take action on social justice issues that have impact on their communities, promoting agency and advocacy.

In this chapter, we will explore how teachers can develop and enhance families and communities in STEAM education through examples from Ms. Young's bilingual English-Spanish class profile (see Table 6.2). Chapter 6 resources on the publisher's companion website provide additional information on the topics discussed in the chapter.

Ms. Young teaches at an urban school serving predominantly immigrant children, many of whom are MLs, in a high-poverty community. Despite limited resources and insufficient support for STEAM education, Ms. Young creatively brings STEAM to life by drawing on the cultural and linguistic knowledge of families and communities. Her goal is not only to

Table 6.2 Class Profile 1

Context	Urban inner-city, high-poverty community, 1st grade, transitional bilingual program where English and Spanish are used for instruction
Teacher	**Ms. Young**, a bilingual Spanish and English teacher

Selected ML Profiles	**Jose**
	• Born in the US to first-generation immigrant parents from Mexico.
	• **Spanish**
	  ◦ Oracy: developing
	  ◦ Literacy: entering
	• **English**
	  ◦ Oracy: emerging
	  ◦ Literacy: emerging
	
	Lyla
	• Born in the US to first-generation Arab American parents.
	• **Arabic**
	  ◦ Oracy: developing
	  ◦ Literacy: entering
	• **English**
	  ◦ Oracy: expanding
	  ◦ Literacy: emerging
	• **Spanish**
	  ◦ Oracy: emerging
	  ◦ Literacy: entering

immerse students in STEAM learning but also to empower families with strategies to support their children's STEAM and overall learning at home.

One of the MLs, Jose, is a six-year-old boy whose parents, Carlos and Sofia, immigrated to the United States from Mexico eight years ago. Carlos is a laborer at his cousin's construction company, while Sofia stays home to care for Jose and his older sister, Maria, a fourth grader at the same school. Ms. Young learns that Sofia, who grew up on a farm in Mexico, has extensive knowledge of organic gardening and enjoys growing vegetables in their small backyard. While Carlos speaks limited English, Sofia primarily communicates in Spanish.

Another student, Lyla, was born in the United States to first-generation immigrant parents from Palestine. Her father, Omar, works at a local grocery store, while her mother, Yasmin, is employed at a community support organization assisting Palestinian and other Middle Eastern immigrants.

Through the experiences of these two families, we will illustrate how Ms. Young engages multilingual families and their broader communities in her STEAM projects, fostering learning and collaboration. Additionally, we will illustrate how her approach to STEAM teaching aligns closely with core principles and key practices in the ESEM Framework introduced in Chapter 2.

What Role Does Family Play in STEAM Education?

Children possess remarkable problem-solving abilities from their earliest years. Starting in infancy, they develop and test intuitive theories about the world around them, much like scientists, by actively exploring their environment through all their senses (Gopnik, 2012). During free play, young children engage with foundational math concepts, exploring patterns, shapes, and spatial relations; comparing sizes; constructing with various materials; and interacting with basic scientific phenomena (Sarama & Clements, 2018). Engaging young children in simple, real-life activities—many of which naturally involve STEAM concepts—during the crucial developmental period leverages their innate curiosity, shapes their brain architecture, and supports cognitive, motor, and language skills (Shonkoff & Phillips, 2000).

Caregivers are children's first and most influential teachers, playing a crucial role in shaping their development. Through everyday activities— such as mixing ingredients while cooking, sorting toys, playing with water, planting seeds, dancing to music, and walking in the woods— families naturally introduce fundamental STEAM concepts like counting, measuring, observing, and grouping. These activities help children make connections between the physical world and abstract ideas (Brenneman, 2011). The home is a dynamic STEAM educational environment because children's learning is deeply rooted in their family's cultural and linguistic context. It is based on meaningful interactions with caregivers and closely tied to their cultural identity and background. This connection is especially important for children from multilingual or multicultural backgrounds, where families can integrate language, culture, and STEAM learning in ways that make it more accessible and relatable (González et al., 2005).

Who Are Our Partners in STEAM Education?

Multilingual Families

The traditional view of STEAM education had a narrow focus on what was taught at school. However, many educators have realized that family involvement, particularly in STEAM subjects, enhances children's academic performance, confidence, and motivation (Salvatierra & Cabello, 2022). Multilingual families, who were once viewed through a deficit ideology that emphasized perceived shortcomings such as limited English proficiency, are now increasingly recognized for their assets and expertise and the systemic inequities they may face (Hoffman et al., 2021). We encourage teachers to reflect on any biases and avoid the common pitfall of engaging with multilingual families from a deficit perspective. By engaging in STEAM activities, multilingual families offer opportunities for dual-language practice, helping children internalize STEAM concepts in both their primary language(s) and the language of instruction. This strengthens the connection between the academic language used in school and the primary language(s), bridging potential language gaps.

Moreover, family involvement makes STEAM education more culturally relevant and accessible, overcoming language barriers and contributing to a more inclusive educational environment. Such collaboration between families and schools fosters more equitable educational practices and ensures better support for all students (Lopez et al., 2022). Schools need to fully recognize the crucial role of families in supporting children's STEAM learning and proactively align STEAM curricula with the meaningful projects and activities already happening at home.

The partnership we envision is a two-way street. On one hand, educators can support families with strategies and resources to further children's STEAM learning. Often, families engage children in activities that are inherently STEAM focused without realizing it, leading to incidental but valuable learning experiences. Some families may not necessarily realize that fostering STEAM skills doesn't require high-tech tools or advanced knowledge; simple, everyday items like pencils, paintbrushes, utensils, magnifying glasses, and building blocks are highly effective for children's learning. As a result, the potential for STEAM learning during early childhood often goes untapped, particularly for underserved children. A "STEAM opportunity gap" exists for children living in poverty or belonging to linguistic and ethnic minority groups, likely due to fewer developmental opportunities at home and in their educational environments (Clements et al., 2016). Family involvement, however, is one of the most powerful tools in addressing these challenges and closing the STEAM opportunity gap. Supporting underresourced and multilingual families to confidently engage in their children's STEAM education is not only an educational priority but also a matter of social justice. On the other hand, educators are encouraged to highlight the cultural and linguistic assets of multilingual families, which contribute to diverse ways of viewing, talking/thinking about, and reasoning through concepts in the STEAM field. This mutual partnership can serve as a powerful avenue for addressing educational inequities and bridging opportunity gaps, helping children access better future job prospects.

Other Community Partners in STEAM Education

In addition to home, informal learning spaces such as museums, libraries, environmental programs, cultural centers, heritage language schools, and community-based organizations offering afterschool, enrichment, and summer programs play an increasingly important role in complementing and enhancing children's school-based STEAM education. This is especially relevant for younger children, who spend about 80% of their waking time in home or informal learning settings during the first five years of life (Meltzoff et al., 2009). The community serves as a rich, dynamic environment for STEAM learning, offering opportunities that schools may not always provide. Community-based STEAM programs give children practical applications of science and engineering practices, enhancing understanding and motivation. Integrating these resources allows schools to extend STEAM learning beyond classroom constraints, offering rich, hands-on experiences that encourage inquiry and exploration.

Community collaborations are essential in providing equitable STEAM education, particularly for underserved communities. Partnerships with local libraries, makerspaces, and museums make STEAM resources more accessible to all students, reducing disparities in educational experiences. This ensures that children from diverse backgrounds have equal opportunities to engage in STEAM learning. Community partnerships also can help build social and cultural connections within STEAM education, especially valuable for culturally and linguistically diverse students. Children learn better when their cultural backgrounds are recognized and integrated into learning. Another benefit of partnerships with local agencies is that they encourage families to participate actively in their children's STEAM learning.

As discussed in Chapter 3, the STEAM learning community encompasses a network of interconnected components working collaboratively toward a shared educational goal. Within this ecosystem, teachers play a key leadership role in initiating partnerships with informal educators—including librarians, museum professionals, afterschool providers, and camp counselors—to enhance students' real-world STEAM experiences. To establish an equity-focused STEAM learning community, teachers can revisit the "STEAM asset mapping" tool introduced in Chapter 3, using it to identify and integrate diverse community resources effectively.

How Do We Develop and Enhance Partnership with Families and Communities?

In this section, we aim to provide pre- and in-service teachers some specific strategies and tools for engaging families and communities in STEAM education (see a template in Table 6.3). Each of these tools and strategies will be explained in more detail.

Table 6.3 Strategies and Tools for Family and Community Partnership

Strategies and Tools	What Does the Mutual Partnership Look Like?
Family as collaborators	
Family workshops	
Educational resources for families	
STEAM family nights	
Family volunteers	
Community engagement	

Families as Collaborators

Teachers invite families to co-create STEAM curricula and involve them in all steps of planning and implementation. In addition, they regularly update families on their children's learning experiences and activities through classroom newsletters, note slips, or weekly updates. This helps families understand what exciting STEAM projects are happening in the classroom and how they can support their children at home. For example, during the spring months, Ms. Young focused her STEAM teaching on plants. She solicited feedback from the classroom families and decided on relevant topics, such as the plant life cycle, photosynthesis, types of plants, their benefits, and gardening techniques, sharing this information with families at the beginning of the term. To engage students, she asked them to draw various flowers and plants to decorate the newsletter, which they brought home to share with their families. As a warm-up activity, she encouraged families to explore their neighborhoods with their children to find and name five different plants. For instance, after dinner, Jose's mother, Sofia, took a walk with him and was excited to discover milkweed flowers, which attract Mexico monarch butterflies. She shared with Jose that monarch butterflies also enjoy *girasoles* (sunflowers) and *vara de oro* (goldenrod). At home, Jose's mother showed him the unique vegetables from Mexico that she had planted in their backyard garden, including *chayote* and *verdolagas* (purslane), which were not often found in the neighborhood grocery stores. Through these experiences, Jose picked up new plant-related vocabulary and gained a deeper connection to his cultural heritage.

Ms. Young used newsletters, emails, and an educational app, ClassDojo, to promote communication with families and students. ClassDojo allowed her to share real-time updates, post student activities, and communicate directly with families. For example, she shared photos and videos of classroom STEAM activities or experiments, helping families stay connected to their child's learning. She also posted STEAM-related challenges for families to try at home, including bilingual instructions and material lists for families to engage with STEAM learning outside of school. ClassDojo offered translation features, which allowed Ms. Young to communicate with multilingual families in their preferred language. This open line of communication supports a collaborative approach to STEAM education, making learning accessible and engaging for all families.

Family Workshops

Co-organized workshops with families specifically focused on STEAM education provide families with simple and effective tips for integrating STEAM concepts into their daily lives. For instance, one idea Ms. Young shared with the families was that while grocery shopping, children can help to weigh produce or calculate prices to strengthen math skills. The primary goal of these workshops is to raise families' awareness of the numerous teachable moments and opportunities present in family life, highlighting the significant role they play in supporting their children's STEAM learning. Teachers convey an important message that engaging in scientific discussions at home can help foster positive identities for children as science learners, enabling them to communicate more effectively about science in their lives.

In one of Ms. Young's co-organized family workshops, she took the lead to use cooking—an everyday activity at home—as an example to demonstrate how families can incorporate STEAM learning. She explained that, while cooking, families can introduce children to basic measurements and chemical reactions. For example, when making corn tortillas, a staple in many Hispanic and Latin American families, a parent or guardian can explain the ingredients (e.g., corn flour, water, and a pinch of salt) and the process of mixing them together to create the dough. Children can participate by measuring ingredients, counting cups of flour, and pressing dough into tortilla shapes using a rolling pin. Ms. Young then invited families to contribute their own ideas connected to STEAM. For instance, Lyla's dad, Omar, shared the STEAM connections while making flatbread, a staple food in Arabic cuisine, using flour, water, salt, and yeast or baking powder. Children can count the number of flatbreads, describe the shape, and observe the dough rising and puffing up from heat. A Korean family suggested that making kimchi offers a way to observe fermentation. This exchange led to a rich and engaging cultural discussion. An everyday cooking activity can evolve into a full-fledged STEAM project, introducing children to diverse concepts and vocabulary, often in their home language.

This approach helps children and families see how science, math, and creativity connect in everyday life.

Workshops can offer families easy-to-implement techniques, such as asking open-ended questions, encouraging observations, promoting hands-on exploration, and documenting findings. At the same time, teachers can learn about different culturally responsive practices and interaction patterns used by families that can be incorporated into the classroom. For example, during a workshop, Ms. Young invited a multilingual parent and child pair to demonstrate how they interacted with each other while the child was testing how fast a toy truck would run on different slopes and textures. After the demonstration, the group discussed the unique cultural and linguistic patterns used by the parent and child. Ms. Young also compared how such patterns were similar or different from the patterns used at school.

Educational Resources for Families

Having access to educational resources is important to families. However, shifting through an abundance of information can also be overwhelming. Therefore, teachers need to familiarize themselves with various STEAM resources, considering the cultural and linguistic backgrounds of the families in the classroom. Families are encouraged to share resources with teachers, especially those that are culturally and linguistically specific. It is important to provide various communication channels, such as text messages, emails, newsletters, online platforms, or educational apps. Utilizing ClassDoJo and parenting blogs can facilitate sharing and discussion between teachers and families.

For instance, to prepare for the plant-focused STEAM project in the spring, Ms. Young collaborated with families to compile a list of age-appropriate, multicultural and multilingual children's books about plants for her first-grade students (see Table 6.4). Ms. Young also planned to document and share the entire process of the plant project with families through the ClassDojo app.

The book collection process inspired Lyla's mother, Yasmin. She joined other families in launching a dual-language book club in their local district. She informed families that they can order books in Arabic,

Table 6.4 Sample Age-Appropriate Children's Books About Plants

Fiction books	• ***The Curious Garden* by Peter Brown.** A beautifully illustrated story about a boy named Liam who discovers a small garden in a city and helps it grow, ultimately transforming his urban environment.
	• ***The Tiny Seed* by Eric Carle.** A classic picture book that follows the journey of a tiny seed as it travels through the seasons and grows into a beautiful flower.
	• **Lola Plants a Garden by Anna McQuinn.** Lola loves to read poems about gardens, so she decides to plant her own. A simple and charming story about planting and patience.
Nonfiction books	• ***From Seed to Plant* by Gail Gibbons.** A detailed yet accessible nonfiction book that introduces young readers to the life cycle of plants, from seeds to germination and growth.
	• ***A Seed Is Sleepy* by Dianna Hutts Aston.** A poetic and scientifically accurate book that celebrates the wonder of seeds, with beautiful illustrations that show their diversity and life cycle.
	• ***What If There Were No Bees?* by Suzanne Slade.** This book explains the importance of bees in pollinating plants and what could happen to plants and ecosystems without them.
Books in other languages, or by authors of various cultures, or with themes of cultural inclusiveness	• ***Las calabacitas de Zoraida/Zoraida's Little Squash* by Francisco X. Alarcón (Spanish and English).** This bilingual story centers on Zoraida's passion for growing squash and her determination to bring them to a town celebration. It beautifully illustrates themes of cultural pride, perseverance, and the joy of gardening.
	• ***¡Siembra una palabra!* [Plant a Seed!] by Judith Anderson and María Jesús Álvarez (Spanish).** This book provides a simple introduction to plant life cycles and the impact of planting. It's ideal for showing children how words, ideas, and plants can grow with care and nurture.
	• ***The Ugly Vegetables* by Grace Lin (English, culturally inclusive).** While this book is in English, it explores the experience of a young girl in an Asian American family growing Chinese vegetables in their garden, which look different from the flowers grown by their neighbors. It's a wonderful way to open discussions about diversity in plants and cultures.

Spanish, or other languages from the local libraries. She made a summer reading list in Arabic for the local library and encouraged the school to put these books on its library wish list.

STEAM Family Nights

STEAM-themed family nights can be organized at a convenient location such as a community center where families can actively engage in hands-on activities with their children. Schools can collaborate with local businesses or organizations to provide workshops or resources for families. For example, Ms. Young invited a local nursery to participate in the STEAM night, where they guided families in building small terrariums using soil, small plants, and decorative elements like rocks and moss. The nursery staff discussed the micro-environment within a terrarium and the water cycle involved. Two bilingual parents provided translation support for families who speak languages other than English and Spanish. Additionally, teachers can use STEAM night to showcase and celebrate children's STEAM activities and achievements, highlighting students' progress and successes during the event.

Family Volunteers

Teachers can invite family members to participate in the classroom and assist with planning and implementing STEAM-related curricular activities as co-facilitator, guest speakers, or volunteers. If available, families can also be invited to join field trips as chaperones to local science museums, technology centers, or engineering firms. For instance, Lyla's mother, Yasmin, recently attended a class trip to Flavorchem, a local company that specializes in creating and manufacturing flavor, fragrance, and ingredient solutions. This established STEAM event has been a collaboration between the school and the company for several years. Yasmin thoroughly enjoyed the trip, took numerous pictures, and was excited to experiment with creating a lemon-flavored cleaning liquid at home with Lyla, using the recipe provided by the company. As part of a follow-up project, Yasmin volunteered to bring in common spices like cinnamon, saffron, cumin, and cardamom, allowing students to explore their textures and aromas. She shared their uses in traditional Arabic cuisine and natural remedies, sparking curiosity about their origins and benefits. Yasmin also explained the cultural significance of essential oils in Arabic traditions, introducing students to how fragrances are used in various aspects of life.

Community Engagement

Teachers can actively map out local community resources and establish connections with outreach or educational coordinators to enrich their curriculum. This can include arranging field trips, inviting community professionals to participate in or cohost school events like STEAM family nights, and collaborating with community agencies to co-develop programs that align with both school and community goals.

Numerous community agencies and programs can provide focused and advanced STEAM resources that schools may not be able to afford. Teachers can cultivate these community resources to expand and enrich children's STEAM learning, making it a community-wide initiative that supports children's wonder and curiosity. For instance, urban museums provided free admission and helped Ms. Young's first graders explore plant life, ecosystems, weather patterns, and animals through hands-on models and multimedia displays. Children can learn about the plant life cycle, habitats, and weather through simulations or live exhibits.

Ms. Young can collaborate with museums to co-design and cohost workshops that explore the intersection of art and science, providing opportunities for children to create nature-inspired crafts, use leaves for printing, or explore geometry in artwork. Building on her plant-focused STEAM project, she used the museum's outdoor botanical garden to engage children in planting seeds, learning about photosynthesis, and tracking plant growth. Museums can also host storytelling sessions featuring books on science and technology topics, such as inventors, astronauts, or animals. Ms. Young can coordinate with the museum to align these themes with her classroom projects.

Many museums have makerspaces where children can engage in creative problem-solving by designing and building their own creations using various materials, such as recycled items, Legos, and art supplies. When families have the opportunities to participate in these activities, their awareness, knowledge, and attitudes toward STEAM education are significantly enhanced.

School Community Garden: A First-Grade STEAM Project Example

As previously mentioned, Ms. Young chose to focus on plants during the spring months in her first-grade classroom. We will use Mr. Young's STEAM project—designing and building a school community garden—as an example to illustrate how she engaged multilingual families and community partners.

The project had multiple goals: (1) students and families were able to design and build a school community garden, integrating elements of botany, environmental science, and engineering; (2) they were able to learn about plant growth, gardening practices, sustainability, composting and recycling (sustainable practices), and environmental protection; and (3) families were able to enhance their awareness of how to support their children's STEAM learning. The project spanned 13 weeks.

The design was age appropriate and practical, utilizing accessible materials to authentically involve multilingual families in STEAM education through familiar, everyday items and cultural knowledge. It showed families that STEAM learning didn't require expensive technology or advanced expertise. It also provided opportunities for families to share their linguistic and cultural assets, making the learning experience more inclusive and relevant for urban, low-income communities. As you review the example, pay attention to the intentions behind each step of the project design.

Below is a planning tool we recommend teachers use to engage families and the community in STEAM projects (Table 6.5). To illustrate its application, we have adapted this tool for the school community garden project as an example.

We elaborate on how Ms. Young used this template for the school community garden project (see Table 6.6). We also include a column to demonstrate how the implementation stages enact the core principles and key practices in the ESEM Framework.

Table 6.5 Template for a Community-Based, STEAM Project Planning Tool

Goal of the Project		
Standards		
Implementation Stage	**STEAM Activities**	**Families and Community Engagement**
Define the problem		
Design a possible solution		
Compare different solutions		
Connection and reflection		

Conclusion

As the world changes, there is growing recognition that STEAM education is essential to prepare children for future challenges. However, STEAM experiences are often concentrated on older children in school settings, leaving limited opportunities for younger children, particularly in home environments and underresourced families. This gap persists despite substantial research showing that early STEAM exposure helps build essential brain architecture and lays the groundwork for lifelong critical-thinking and learning skills. Bridging this gap requires innovative collaboration among educators, families, and community partners to nurture the inventors and problem-solvers of tomorrow.

Ms. Young's gardening project exemplifies how STEAM initiatives can engage children and families from diverse backgrounds, honoring the cultural and linguistic strengths that multilingual families bring. It is crucial for teachers to sincerely involve families as true partners, respect their unique contributions, and intentionally align the school curriculum with home experiences. Educators need to hold the belief that all families want the best for their children and are capable of supporting their learning, including in STEAM subjects. At the same time, teachers are encouraged to remain attentive to the strengths, needs, and potential anxieties of immigrant and multilingual parents, advocating for the resources and support these families need to succeed.

Table 6.6 Planning Tool of School Community Garden

Goal of the Project	To establish a school community garden, engaging students, families, and the community in a culturally inclusive project that fosters learning in STEAM, sustainability, and cultural pride.		
Standards	K-ESS3-2, NCAS Va Pr 6, WIDA ELD-SC.1.Explain.Interpretive, ELD-SC.1.Explain.Expressive		
Implementation Stage	**STEAM Activities**	**Families and Community Engagement**	**Enacted Core Principles and Key Practices Focusing on P1 and P4**
Define the problem	• At the beginning of the project, Ms. Young sent a flyer, co-designed by students, to inform families about the garden project. The flyer detailed the topics, timelines, and student involvement. • Ms. Young researched different plants/vegetables from different cultures and made some suggestions to students. At the same time, she conducted a survey with students and families to decide which practical or culturally unique plants (flowers and vegetables) they would like to grow. The yard space was measured, and a decision was made to limit the planting to around 20 species.	• Families provided input on which plants to grow, contributing to the final selection of flowers and vegetables. • Families helped their children name and identify six different plants in their neighborhood. • Jose's mom, Sophia, who had extensive botanical knowledge, led a community nature walk for the whole class. Sophia used Spanish for the nature walk, and Ms. Young assisted with translation as necessary.	P1.1 Ensure that curriculum content is relevant, inclusive, and accessible to all students.

Table 6.6 (*Continued*)

Implementation Stage	STEAM Activities	Families and Community Engagement	Enacted Core Principles and Key Practices Focusing on P1 and P4
Design a possible solution	• Ms. Young organized a class field trip to a local botanical garden, where children learned about garden design, seasonal plant selection, and sustainable gardening practices. • After the field trip, students discussed garden layouts and tools, incorporating mathematical concepts like symmetry, patterns, and spatial reasoning. Each student submitted a graphic proposal, and the class voted on a final garden layout.	• Families were invited to attend the field trip as chaperones and were provided free passes. • Families supported the garden design process by providing input on plants and necessary tools.	P4.1 Foster a classroom culture that respects each other, values critical thinking, and builds community—encourages teamwork and critical thinking through collaborative garden design.
Compare different solutions	• Selected a final garden layout based on class voting after reviewing student graphic proposals.	• Families provided additional input on the layout design and tool requirements, leveraging their practical gardening experience. • Families received a curated list of culturally inclusive books centered on themes related to plants. • Jose's mother, Sofia, volunteered to read to children the book *Las calabacitas de Zoraida/Zoraida's Little Squash* by Francisco X. Alarcón. She supported children's discussion on cultural pride, perseverance, and the joy of gardening.	P1.2 Design learning units that are informed by standards and critical issues in the local and global communities. P1.5 Implement teaching strategies that recognize and value MLs' linguistic and cultural assets.

(Continued)

Table 6.6 (*Continued*)

Implementation Stage	STEAM Activities	Families and Community Engagement	Enacted Core Principles and Key Practices Focusing on P1 and P4
Planting	• Students participated in garden bed setup and planting and decorated garden walls, rocks, and labels with artwork.	• Families made significant contributions by donating rain barrels, watering cans, sprinklers, and compost bins. They also helped to secure donations from local businesses with soil, fertilizer, and garden boxes. • Lyla's father, Omar, who works at a grocery store, helped secure donations of seeds for the project, while Carlos, Jose's father, and other families volunteered their time to assist in assembling raised beds and garden structures.	P1.1 Ensure that curriculum content is relevant, inclusive, and accessible to all students.
Ongoing maintenance and monitoring	• Ms. Young scheduled the children to rotate in caring for the garden, with tasks such as watering, weeding, and pruning. • Students regularly documented plant growth through measurements, drawings, and photographs. These observations were shared with parents via ClassDoJo and the classroom Facebook group. • Lessons focused on composting, soil health, and water conservation, using compost bins and rain barrels for sustainability.	• Families volunteered for ongoing garden maintenance, such as weeding and watering, by signing up for specific tasks. • Family volunteers helped collect food waste from the school cafeteria, recorded the weight of the waste, and helped to raise students' awareness about the importance of reducing food waste. • Lyla's mother, Yasmin, volunteered to read a book on food waste to the class, *Waste Not, Want Not* by Brenda Shannon Yee. This book introduces young readers to the concept of food waste.	P4.3 Facilitate collaborative learning experiences that promote critical inquiry, evaluate multiple perspectives, and build empathy. P4.5 Encourage MLs to take action on social justice issues impacting their communities, promoting agency and advocacy.

Table 6.6 (Continued)

Implementation Stage	STEAM Activities	Families and Community Engagement	Enacted Core Principles and Key Practices Focusing on P1 and P4
Connection and reflection	• The children made poster presentations about the garden project, and bilingual students were encouraged to make posters in their native languages. • Students wrote thank-you notes to their parents, which were displayed in ClassDojo. • Ms. Young planned a follow-up art show in the fall, encouraging children to create art using leaves and other garden materials. Children were also invited to display garden- or flower-related artwork from their cultural backgrounds, such as Chinese paper cutting or Islamic geometric floral patterns.	• Family volunteers organized a fresh veggie stand as a community event. • Family volunteers shared different dishes and recipes using the same vegetable, tomatoes, demonstrating a variety of cultural dishes. Examples included pasta sauce, salsa, tomato salad, and egg with tomato stir-fry. • Families were also invited to collaborate on the fall art show with their children, contributing to the cultural dimension of the project. • Family feedback was solicited for planning the next STEAM project, ensuring ongoing family involvement.	P1.3 Develop learning experiences that reflect and build on the cultural and linguistic assets of MLs. P1.4 Provide opportunities for MLs to see themselves reflected positively in the curriculum. P 4.2 Encourage MLs to critically examine issues of power, privilege, and inequality in a disciplinary context.

References

Brenneman, K. (2011). Science in the early years: Policies and practices. *Early Childhood Research & Practice, 13*(1).

Clements, D. H., Sarama, J., & Germeroth, C. (2016). Learning executive function and early mathematics: Directions of causal relations. *Early Childhood Research Quarterly, 36*(3), 79–90. https://doi.org/10.1016/j.ecresq.2015.12.009

González, N., Moll, L., & Amanti, C. (2005). *Funds of knowledge: Theorizing practices in households, communities, and classrooms.* Routledge.

Gopnik, A. (2012). Scientific thinking in young children: Theoretical advances, empirical research, and policy implications. *Science, 337*(6102), 1623–1627.

Hoffman, L., Suh, E., & Zollman, A. (2021). What STEM teachers need to know and do to engage families of emergent multilingual students (English language learners). *Journal of STEM Teacher Education, 56*(1), 1–15.

Lopez, A., Deitrick, L., & De la Rosa, A. (2022). Culturally responsive STEAM education: Engaging multilingual learners through family partnerships. *Journal of Early Childhood Literacy, 22*(3), 481–500.

Meltzoff, A. N., Kuhl, P. K., Movellan, J., & Sejnowski, T. J. (2009). Foundations for a new science of learning. *Science, 325*(5938), 284–288. https://doi.org/10.1126/science.1175626

National Academies of Sciences, Engineering, and Medicine. (2018). *How people learn II: Learners, contexts, and cultures.* National Academies Press. DOI:10.17226/24783

Salvatierra, L., & Cabello, V. M. (2022). Starting at home: What does the literature indicate about parental involvement in early childhood STEM education? *Education Science, 12*, 218. https://doi.org/10.3390/educsci12030218

Sarama, J., & Clements, D. H. (2018). Promoting positive transitions through coherent instruction, assessment, and professional development: The TRIAD scale-up model. In A. J. Mashburn, J. LoCasale-Crouch, & K. Pears (Eds.), *Kindergarten readiness* (pp. 327–348). Springer.

Shonkoff, J. P., & Phillips, D. A. (Eds.). (2000). *From neurons to neighborhoods: The science of early childhood development.* National Academies Press.

7

Selecting and Integrating Technology to Enhance MLs' STEAM Learning

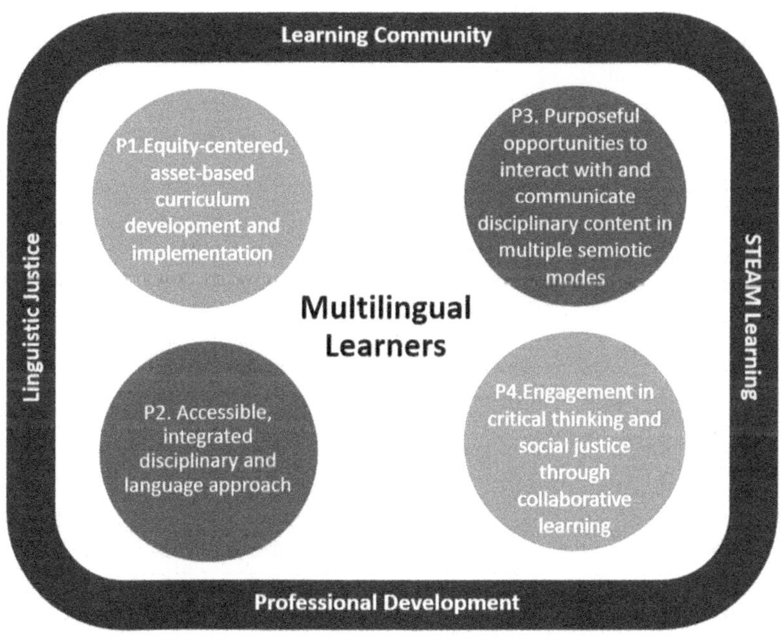

Figure 7.1 ESEM Framework

Table 7.1 Focused Core Principles and Key Teaching Practices in ESEM Framework

Focused Core Principles	Key Teaching Practices
P2. Accessible, integrated disciplinary and language approach	P2.1 Provide explicit instruction on how languages and culture work for disciplines. P2.2 Scaffold language use in disciplinary contexts, supporting MLs' comprehension and expression throughout investigations. P2.3 Facilitate repeated exposure to and practice of language within meaningful disciplinary contexts. P2.4 Provide opportunities for MLs to engage in disciplinary practices (such as scientific inquiry and mathematical problem-solving) by using their language skills. P2.5 Promote translanguaging as a valid language practice that supports MLs' learning across disciplines.
P3. Purposeful opportunities to interact with and communicate disciplinary content in multiple semiotic modes	P3.1 Design interactive learning experiences that immerse MLs in a diverse range of semiotic modes. P3.2 Provide differentiated multimodal disciplinary content adaptive to MLs' learning preferences and linguistic needs. P3.3 Integrate technology tools and sense-making resources that support MLs' engagement with disciplinary content. P3.4 Scaffold MLs' use of multiple semiotic modes to express their understanding of disciplinary concepts and communicate their ideas effectively. P3.5 Encourage MLs to create and share multimodal projects that demonstrate their understanding of disciplinary concepts and skills and enhanced proficiency in multiple languages.

Technology is a key component of STEAM education. This chapter discusses technology, but the primary focus is to support STEAM educators to select and integrate technology as tools to effectively plan and deliver instruction and enhance MLs' learning. Chapter 7 resources on the publisher's companion website provide additional information on technology. This chapter situates scenarios and examples based on Class Profile 3 (see Table 7.2).

Situated at a school in a rural area in southern Illinois, Ms. Nowak centered the STEAM curriculum around students' interest and community assets. She sparked her fifth graders' scientific curiosity by immersing

Table 7.2 Class Profile 3

Context	**Rural, 5th grade, content-based language instruction model**
Teacher	**Ms. Nowak**, a Polish and English bilingual mainstream classroom teacher who immigrated with her family to the US in her teen years

Selected ML Profiles	**Allin**
	• Born in Angola with Umbundu- and Portuguese-speaking parents. The family moved to the US when she was four years old. Allin is at risk of becoming a long-term English learner (L-TEL).
	• **Umbundu:**
	  ○ Oracy: developing
	  ○ Literacy: entering
	• **Portuguese:**
	  ○ Oracy: developing
	  ○ Literacy: entering
	• **English**
	  ○ Oracy: bridging
	  ○ Literacy: developing
	
	Mario
	• Born in Venezuela and had interrupted schooling while the family fled political turmoil and economic collapse before immigrating to the US. Mario is considered a student with interrupted or limited formal education (SIFE).
	• **Spanish:**
	  ○ Oracy: developing
	  ○ Literacy: entering
	• **English**
	  ○ Oracy: expanding
	  ○ Literacy: developing

them in the captivating world of butterflies through the "Fly, Butterfly" project. By starting the unit with a short video of the monarch butterfly's migration, Ms. Nowak prompted discussions about their destination and lifespan, initiating the students' exploration of butterflies. She established a monarch butterfly observation corner in her classroom, allowing students to witness firsthand the life cycles of these remarkable insects. Complementing this practical experience, Ms. Nowak collected butterfly-themed books (available in paper and digital versions), including bilingual children's books such as *Senorita Mariposa* (Gundersheimer, 2019, bilingual Spanish and English edition), *Lotli the Monarch Butterfly* (Romo-

Rabago & Torres, n.d., bilingual Spanish and English edition), *Butterfly: The Life Cycle of the Painted Lady* (Adefris, 2024, bilingual Portuguese and English edition), and *Velma Gratch and the Way Cool Butterfly* (Madison, 2012). The inclusion of MLs' primary languages, simplified language choices and structures, rich visuals, and audio recordings for these books enhances students' content understanding while fostering language development and literacy skills. Additionally, Ms. Nowak asked students to participate in the flower garden projects to plant more milkweed for butterfly habitats. Upon the butterflies being ready to fly away, the class held a big celebration with families, allowing students to share what they had learned.

The above scenario demonstrates examples of Ms. Nowak empowering her students to construct knowledge collaboratively and communicate learning creatively by supplementing hands-on, experiential learning with appropriate technology tools. As technology evolves and advances, teachers may feel overwhelmed with so many new tools. They need guidance on articulating the purposes of technology and identifying criteria to select and integrate appropriate technological tools effectively for all students. In the first part of this chapter, we explore the considerations for technology integration and digital literacies in diverse classrooms, followed by a discussion of technology standards and technological frameworks. In the second part of the chapter, we share an ML-focused technology evaluation tool to help educators assess the selection and use of technology. A sample technology-enhanced activity is used to elaborate how to implement the core principles and key teaching practices from the ESEM Framework. In the final part of the chapter, we discuss the potentials and limitations of AI tools for STEAM teachers to support MLs.

What Are Considerations for Technology Integration and Digital Literacies in Diverse Classrooms?

Ziegler and González-Lloret (2022) identify three key characteristics of technology: accessibility, social interaction, and affordances. These characteristics have direct implications for technology use in classrooms. The first addresses equity by emphasizing that technology must be accessible to everyone. One way to ensure accessibility is that each student has access to a digital device and a reliable internet connection. Second, to counter the notion that interacting with technology is isolating, teachers can leverage its features to support telecollaboration and networking. Many technology tools embed features that support virtual collaboration. Google Docs, for instance, allows multiple learners to collaborate on the same document despite their different physical locations. Lastly, teachers clearly identify the affordances of technology based on students' needs. Affordances refers to what technology brings to the learning environment and how it shapes the content and its medium–language. For example, technology can enhance both language development and content learning for MLs. Apps like Google Translate facilitate comprehension and communication by allowing MLs to translate between their primary language(s) and English. Additionally, online platforms like PhET (https:// phet.colorado.edu/) offer free interactive simulations for various STEM subjects, promoting content learning through hands-on investigation and data collection to build scientific explanations. However, while new digital tools may initially engage and excite students, teachers need to pay attention to novelty effects, which can wear off over time, potentially reducing tools' long-term impact on teaching and learning (Ziegler & González-Lloret, 2022).

Further, all students need to demonstrate competence in digital literacies to effectively navigate, evaluate, create, and communicate information in digital environments. But what do digital literacies encompass? Tour (2020) cautions that digital literacy practices for MLs tend to focus narrowly on basic technical skills. This approach overlooks the broader range of needs that MLs have, which includes not only technological proficiency but also language development, sociocultural understanding, pragmatic application, and critical literacy skills.

Informed by the discussion above, major considerations for teachers to integrate technology and teach digital literacies in classrooms with MLs include the following:

- How can technology play a role in bringing social learning experiences to MLs?
- How can technology enhance the learning process (tailoring content/cognitive burden/language) for MLs?
- How does the experience contribute to MLs' development of digital literacies?

What Are Technology Standards?

In this section, we will review the ISTE and TESOL standards to explore how instructional technology should be integrated for MLs.

ISTE Standards

The International Society for Technology in Education (ISTE) is a nonprofit organization that articulates standards for the use of technology in classrooms and schools. The ISTE standards provide a framework for stakeholders such as educators, leaders, and instructional technology coaches to effectively use technology in order to create high-impact, sustainable, flexible, and equitable learning experiences (ISTE, 2024). A set of ISTE standards is also created for students. These standards are recognized and adopted across all US states and numerous countries globally. In this book, we will primarily focus on ISTE standards for educators and students.

The ISTE standards for educators and students are broken down into different roles they respectively play in the teaching and learning process (see Table 7.3).

TESOL Technology Standards

The TESOL international association created technology standards (TESOL, 2008), which offer guidance for learners, educators, and administrators who integrate technology to enhance English language

Table 7.3 ISTE (2024) Standards for Educators and Students

ISTE Standards for *Educators*	ISTE Standards for *Students*
Learner	Empowered learner
Leader	Digital citizen
Citizen	Knowledge constructor
Collaborator	Innovative designer
Designer	Computational thinker
Facilitator	Creative communicator
Analyst	Global collaborator

Table 7.4 TESOL (2008) Technology Standard Goals for Language Teachers and Language Learners

TESOL Technology Standard Goals for *Language Teachers*	TESOL Technology Standard Goals for *Language Learners*
Acquire and maintain foundational knowledge and skills in technology	Demonstrate foundational knowledge and skills in technology for a multilingual world
Integrate pedagogical knowledge and skills with technology to enhance language teaching and learning	Use technology in socially and culturally appropriate, legal, and ethical ways
Apply technology in record-keeping, feedback, and assessment	Effectively use and critically evaluate technology-based tools as aids in the development of language learning competence as part of formal instruction and for further learning
Use technology to improve communication, collaboration, and efficiency	

learning and teaching. The standards are categorized by goals for language teachers and language learners, respectively (see Table 7.4). The goals are further broken down into specific standards.

When comparing the ISTE and TESOL technology standards, there are several common themes. For example, both emphasize digital literacies/citizenship and teachers' professional development. However, there are also some differences. One is that ISTE includes standards for multiple stakeholders, while TESOL articulates technology standards specifically for teachers and learners. Additionally, the focus of these two standards diverges. ISTE, as a leading organization specializing in technology integration in education, places a broader emphasis on how to use technology effectively to enhance learning experiences. In contrast, TESOL, as a leading organization focusing on teaching English to speakers of other languages, strongly focuses on implementing technology to support language and literacy development for MLs. All teachers are language teachers, as language is an essential part of introducing, processing, and applying content (TESOL Writing Team, 2018). When it comes to working with MLs, both standards should be considered and incorporated to create technology objectives for students. In other words, the instructional purpose of selecting and using technology as tools is to facilitate content development and support language learning simultaneously.

What Are Technology Frameworks and Their Connection to WIDA?

Several research-based technology frameworks have been developed to guide technology integration in education. We will first introduce three frameworks in this section: the SAMR model (Puentedura, 2013), TPACK (Mishra & Koehler, 2006), and the Triple E framework (Kolb, 2019). We will then briefly discuss the connection among the presented technology frameworks to WIDA (2020). A comparative analysis of these frameworks will lead to a practical evaluation tool that guides teachers in selecting and using technology with MLs.

The SAMR model (Puentedura, 2013) consists of four levels that indicate how technology can be integrated in instruction to impact teaching and learning. Each letter in the model corresponds to one of the levels.

S stands for substitution, which means that technology serves as a substitute with no functional improvement. An example is that instead of working on a traditional paper worksheet, students work on a digital copy.

A stands for augmentation, which not only substitutes traditional learning tasks but also has functional improvement. One example is that digital books have read-aloud features that support MLs' reading comprehension.

M stands for modification, which indicates that technology enables teachers to redesign tasks significantly. For instance, students are able to collaborate on Google Docs and receive instant feedback.

R stands for redefinition, which means that teachers are able to create new learning tasks that were impossible without technology. For example, teachers can set up videoconferencing with insect specialists from different parts of the world to share their research on monarch butterfly migration with the students.

We represent the four levels in the SAMR model using the analogy of telecommunication tools in Figure 7.2.

The SAMR model is helpful for teachers to assess how their technology use impacts learning tasks. However, it does not directly connect technology to learning goals. The other two, TPACK (Mishra & Koehler, 2006) and the Triple E framework (Kolb, 2019), provide guidance for teachers to situate technology use in the broader context of teaching and learning. TPACK stands for technology, pedagogy, and content knowledge.

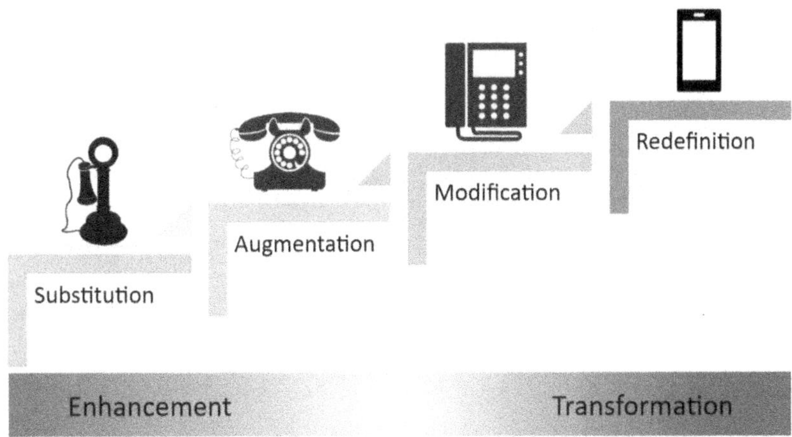

Figure 7.2 The SAMR Model

The underlying assumption for TPACK is that teachers need three types of knowledge to be effective: knowledge about the subject area (content), the ways they teach the content (pedagogy), and knowledge about digital tools (technology). TPACK centers on how these three types of knowledge intersect with each other and contribute to teaching. It emphasizes that the effectiveness of using technology should be assessed beyond specific learning tasks.

In comparison with the other frameworks, Triple E (Kolb, 2019) is a student-centered framework that focuses on assessing how teachers integrate technology to support students to achieve learning goals. The three Es in the framework are engagement, enhancement, and extension. This framework can be converted to a rubric (https://www.tripleeframework.com/triple-e-evaluation-rubric-for-lesson-design.html) with a list of self-evaluation questions for teachers, centering on examining whether technology helps students to engage in learning goals, enhances their understanding of the learning goals, and extends learning beyond the school to their life. Due to the abovementioned features, the Triple E framework is recommended for teachers to examine their effectiveness of using technology in their classrooms.

Connection to WIDA

We introduced the WIDA ELD Framework (2020) in Chapter 1. The WIDA ELD Framework aims to promote equity for MLs by guiding teachers on how to support the social, instructional, and academic language students need for engaging with peers, educators, and school curricula (WIDA, 2020). This means that teachers should consider technology tools not only from the perspectives of what to teach (content) and how to teach it (pedagogy), but also in terms of how these tools facilitate meaningful and intentional language use by engaging MLs in activities that are authentic to STEM professionals. Therefore, the WIDA Framework guides teachers to examine how language is used in the context of meaningful content and to develop support for MLs to use the language to achieve the learning objectives. You can find a summary of the alignment among the presented technology standards, frameworks, and WIDA connections in Table 7.5.

Implementation Guide

To design effective technology-enhanced lessons, teachers can employ the SAMR or TPACK model to evaluate and integrate technology. By applying ISTE and TESOL standards, teachers can clearly define the roles and competencies required for both educators and students in technology use. They can utilize the Triple E framework to ensure that technology not only engages students but also enhances and extends their learning experiences. Further, teachers should align technology integration with WIDA standards to support the language and content development of MLs, ensuring that their educational needs are met through thoughtful and strategic use of technology.

Based on the recommendations from the technology frameworks and the WIDA (2014) ELD standards and resource guide, we present a technology evaluation checklist in Table 7.6 that supports teachers to select and integrate technology for MLs' language development and content learning. The evaluation checklist is organized by the categories of technology tool, language, content, and individual. Further, the content category is broken down into three criteria highlighted in the Triple E framework—namely, engagement, enhancement, and extension.

When selecting a technology tool, it is essential to evaluate its capabilities through the lens of the SAMR and Triple E frameworks to determine its effectiveness in transforming and enhancing learning experiences. Teachers can assess whether the tool supports MLs' language development in alignment with TESOL and WIDA standards. Further, TPACK and ISTE standards alignment sheds light on how the tool enriches content

Table 7.5 Alignment Among Technology Standards, Frameworks, and WIDA

Domain	ISTE Standards	TESOL Technology Standards	SAMR Model	TPACK Framework	Triple E Framework	WIDA Standards
Educator Roles	Learner, Leader, Citizen, Collaborator, Designer, Facilitator, Analyst	Teacher Goal 1: Acquire and maintain foundational knowledge and skills in technology	Substitution, augmentation, modification, redefinition	Technology, pedagogy, content knowledge intersection	Engagement, enhancement, extension	Language development strategies
Student Roles	Empowered Learner, Digital Citizen, Knowledge Constructor, Innovative Designer, Computational Thinker, Global Collaborator	Student Goal 1: Demonstrate foundational knowledge and skills in technology for a multilingual world	Substitution, augmentation, modification, redefinition	Intersection applied to student-centered learning	Focus on enhancing and extending student learning	Focus on using language for content learning
Technology Integration Levels	Focus on how to integrate technology across various teaching and learning activities	Teacher Goal 2: Integrate pedagogical knowledge and skills with technology to enhance language teaching and learning	Substitution, augmentation, modification, redefinition	Situates technology within the broader context of education	Guides the effectiveness of technology in reaching learning goals	Technology facilitates meaningful and intentional language use
Language Learning	Emphasizes equitable access to technology to support learning	Teacher Goal 4: Use technology in socially and culturally appropriate, legal, and ethical ways	Links technology use to specific learning outcomes	Incorporates language teaching within content learning	Emphasizes critical thinking and problem-solving	Emphasizes the role of technology in language development
Content Learning	Focus on content-specific technology use	Teacher Goal 4: Apply technology to enhance content learning	Connects technology to content-specific learning goals	Aligns content knowledge with technology and pedagogy	Extends learning beyond the classroom	Guides content teaching with a language development focus

Table 7.6 ML-Focused Technology Evaluation Checklist

Technology Tool

Accessibility: Is the technology accessible in and outside of school? Is it compatible with different devices and operational systems? Does it work with and without internet access?

Cultural and linguistic responsiveness: Does the technology offer content and learning opportunities that reflect diverse cultural and linguistic experiences without bias?

Navigation, organization, and customization: Does the technology provide intuitive navigation, clear organization, adaptable content, and multimodal output and input?

Language	Content

Language

- Is the purpose of using the technology clearly explained to MLs using comprehensible language?
- Are the technical terms and features easy for MLs to comprehend?
- Does the technology support the development of various language domains (e.g., speaking, listening, reading, and writing)?
- Does the activity elicit or practice one or more key language uses (e.g., explain, argue, narrate, and inform) and registers?
- Does the activity allow MLs to use all their linguistic resources (translanguaging)?

Content

Engagement
- Is the technology use and learning goals aligned?
- Does the technology motivate MLs to actively engage with the content?
- Do the technical features in the technology keep MLs focused on the learning goals?
- Does the technology engage MLs in collaborative learning?

Enhancement
- Are there multiple ways for MLs to explore and understand the content?
- Does the technology provide multiple opportunities with meaningful and immediate feedback for MLs to meet learning goals?
- Does the technology include multimodal and multilingual features for MLs to demonstrate their understanding of the learning goals?

Extension
- Does the activity connect classroom learning with MLs' daily lives and experiences?
- Does the technology support MLs' continuous learning beyond the classroom?
- Does the activity provide real-life applications meaningful to MLs?
- Does the activity help MLs develop digital literacy competence?

Individual

- Is the technology suitable for the age and development level of the MLs?
- Does it provide appropriate levels of stimulation?
- Could the activity trigger any negative feelings or memories?
- Does the technology adapt to individual MLs' needs and learning levels?

Adapted from Fairbairn & Jones-Vo (2010).

learning. Finally, it is important to consider individual learner needs, especially for MLs, so that the tool supports their unique requirements as detailed in the WIDA framework. This comprehensive evaluation checklist ensures that the technology tool is both pedagogically sound and inclusive. While it may seem overwhelming at first, we designed this tool with the purpose of encouraging STEAM teachers, in collaboration with other staff members such as the ESL teacher and the technology coach, to engage in the process of selecting and using technology to help MLs reach their fullest potential.

What Does Technology Integration Look Like in the Classroom?

In this section, we will use one example to demonstrate how selecting and integrating technology connects to the core principles in the ESEM Framework. Although all the principles are applicable, we will focus on the two most relevant principles highlighted in Table 7.1. These principles are P2: Accessible, integrated disciplinary and language approach; and P3: Purposeful opportunities to interact with and communicate disciplinary content in multiple semiotic modes. We will also elaborate on how the key teaching practices related to Principles 2 and 3 are put into action with technology-enhanced instructional activities.

Technology Selection and Integration Example

Ms. Nowak evaluated the Seesaw app (https://seesaw.com/) using the provided technology evaluation checklist (see Table 7.7). While evaluating the tool for MLs, Ms. Nowak also paid special attention to features that specifically address the needs of MLs' families.

Based on the results of the evaluation checklist, she adopted the Seesaw app for students to create their final presentations in the "Fly, Butterfly" unit, through which they shared their project journey and findings with the school community. See Table 7.8 for how the activities that leverage specific Seesaw app features address the core principles and key teaching practices in the ESEM Framework.

Table 7.7 Sample ML-Focused Technology Evaluation Checklist

Technology Tool: Seesaw App

Accessibility: Is the technology accessible in and outside of school? (*Yes*) Is it compatible with different devices and operational systems? (*Yes*) Does it work with and without internet access? (*Only works with internet access*)

Cultural and linguistic responsiveness: Does the technology offer content and learning opportunities that reflect diverse cultural and linguistic experiences without bias? (*Yes, teachers can create, curate, and share the culturally and linguistically responsive content*)

Navigation, organization, and customization: Does the technology provide intuitive navigation, clear organization, adaptable content, and multimodal output and input? (*Yes, for the most part; may require some orientation for young children or less tech-savvy families*)

Language	Content
• Is the purpose of using the technology clearly explained to MLs using comprehensible language? (*Yes*) • Are the technical terms and features easy for MLs to comprehend? (*Yes, with multimodal and multilingual support*) • Does the technology support the development of various language domains (e.g., speaking, listening, reading, and writing)? (*Yes, with teacher customizable activities*) • Does the activity elicit or practice one or more key language uses (e.g., explain, argue, narrate, and inform) and registers? (*Yes, with teacher customizable activities*) • Does the activity allow MLs to use all their linguistic resources (translanguaging)? (*Yes, with multimodal and teacher customizable tasks*)	**Engagement** • Is the technology use and learning goals aligned? (*Yes, with teacher customizable activities for specific learning goals*) • Does the technology motivate MLs to actively engage with the content? (*Yes*) • Do the technical features in the technology keep MLs focused on the learning goals? (*Yes*) • Does the technology engage MLs in collaborative learning? (*Yes, through collaborative activities and peer feedback*) **Enhancement** • Are there multiple ways for MLs to explore and understand the content? (*Yes*) • Does the technology provide multiple opportunities with meaningful and immediate feedback for MLs to meet learning goals? (*Yes*) • Does the technology include multimodal and multilingual features for MLs to demonstrate their understanding of the learning goals? (*Yes*) **Extension** • Does the activity connect classroom learning with MLs' daily lives and experiences? (*Yes*) • Does the technology support MLs' continuous learning beyond the classroom? (*Yes, with access outside of the classroom*) • Does the activity provide real-life applications meaningful to MLs? (*Yes*) • Does the activity help MLs develop digital literacy competence? (*Yes, with different tasks MLs engage in*)

Individual

- Is the technology suitable for the age and development level of the MLs? (*Yes, Seesaw is user friendly and appropriate for a range of age and developmental levels*)
- Does it provide appropriate levels of stimulation? (*Yes, with engaging and interactive activities*)
- Could the activity trigger any negative feelings or memories? (*Unlikely*)
- Does the technology adapt to individual MLs' needs and learning levels? (*Yes, for differentiated activities tailored to match learners' interests and needs*)

Table 7.8 Implementing Core Principles and Key Teaching Practices Through Seesaw

Seesaw for Final Project	Enacted Sample Core Principles and Key Teaching Practices
- Seesaw's interface supports multimodal directions and content presentation. Directions or content can be provided in written or spoken form (through recordings) with visual support. This ensures that MLs can understand expectations and access content without feeling lost. Ms. Nowak recorded the presentation guidelines in English, Spanish, and Portuguese, and also provided an example of a completed presentation.	P2.2 Scaffold language use in disciplinary contexts, supporting MLs' comprehension and expression throughout investigations. P3.2 Provide differentiated multimodal disciplinary content adaptive to MLs' learning preferences and linguistic needs. P3.3 Integrate technology tools and sense-making resources that support MLs' engagement with disciplinary content. P3.4 Scaffold MLs' use of multiple semiotic modes to express their understanding of disciplinary concepts and communicate their ideas effectively.
- Seesaw allows teachers to embed various language supports for MLs, such as word banks, sentence and paragraph stems, and graphic organizers. This enables students to access the language tools they need as they work on their projects. In addition to utilizing these features in Seesaw, Ms. Nowak also paired students during the brainstorming and drafting phases of their projects. Allin and Mario each had a partner	P2.3 Use content-based instruction to teach language skills within meaningful disciplinary contexts. P3.2 Provide differentiated multimodal disciplinary content adaptive to MLs' learning preferences and linguistic needs. P3.3 Integrate technology tools and sense-making resources that support MLs' engagement with disciplinary content.

(Continued)

Table 7.8 (*Continued*)

Seesaw for Final Project	Enacted Sample Core Principles and Key Teaching Practices
• who shared their primary language and was at a higher proficiency level in English, providing additional support and collaboration as they developed their presentations. The partners engaged in a peer review before they finalized their project.	
• MLs have the flexibility to present their learning in multimodal formats, allowing their multilingual voices to be captured and showcased. For instance, Allin created a bilingual informational picture book with voice-over narration, while Mario produced a video where he explained the migration journey of monarch butterflies using his detailed drawings and written text in both Spanish and English.	P2.5 Promote translanguaging as a valid language practice that supports MLs' learning across disciplines. P3.3 Integrate technology tools and sense-making resources that support MLs' engagement with disciplinary content. P3.5 Encourage MLs to create and share multimodal projects that demonstrate their understanding of disciplinary concepts and skills and enhanced proficiency in multiple languages.
• Seesaw enables teachers and peers to provide timely feedback in various formats (text, voice, and video) as students work on their projects. This feedback accommodates different language needs and helps MLs refine and improve their work.	P2.4 Provide opportunities for MLs to engage in disciplinary practices (such as scientific inquiry and mathematical problem-solving) by using their language skills. P3.3 Integrate technology tools and sense-making resources that support MLs' engagement with disciplinary content. P3.4 Scaffold MLs' use of multiple semiotic modes to express their understanding of disciplinary concepts and communicate their ideas effectively.

Most important of all, Seesaw is free for families to join using the invitation code provided by the teacher. It offers a way for families to stay connected with their child's learning. The app's built-in translation features for messages and posts help eliminate language barriers, enabling diverse families to communicate directly with teachers and vice versa. Overall, this example elaborates why Seesaw was an appropriate and effective tool and how the designed activities empowered MLs to activate their cultural and linguistic resources, facilitate content and language learning, inspire creativity, and engage family participation.

How Do We Use AI in STEAM Education for MLs?

Brief Introduction of AI and NLP

Artificial intelligence (AI) is an emerging technology wave that transforms modern life and education. AI is defined as "systems that use hardware, algorithms, and data to create 'intelligence' to do things like make decisions, discover patterns, and perform some sort of action" (Ruiz & Fusco, n.d.). AI systems can perform tasks such as cooking and driving that were typically performed by human intelligence. As a branch of AI, a natural language processor (NLP) such as ChatGPT enables computers to comprehend, interpret, and generate human language based on the input they receive. By processing language data, an NLP can engage in conversations, answer questions, translate languages, and perform various language-related tasks. AI tools open new opportunities for teachers to enhance teaching effectiveness and support diverse learners with varied needs.

Benefits of Using AI Tools

Rather than focusing on teaching elementary students how to use AI, this section elaborates on how STEAM educators can foster enhanced learning outcomes for their MLs by leveraging AI to adapt instruction efficiently and effectively. Using AI in instructional planning for MLs offers several benefits for educators (How & Hung, 2019; Huynh & Gonzalez, 2024; Muhisn et al., 2019; Tang et al., 2023; Xu & Ouyang, 2022). The benefits include but are not limited to (1) overcoming language barriers with MLs and their families through translation; (2) providing personalized learning pathways that meet MLs' linguistic needs and build on their background knowledge; (3) making STEAM learning contextualized and culturally responsive; (4) developing adaptive learning based on student assessment data; and (5) facilitating collaboration among all the partners.

First, AI-powered tools like real-time translators (e.g., Google Translate and Microsoft Translator) facilitate immediate translation of instructional materials, teacher instructions, and student questions, helping MLs understand complex STEAM concepts without language barriers. Additionally, AI-driven language models can interpret and translate live conversations during class, enabling students to actively participate and engage with their peers and teachers.

Second, AI systems can adapt to individual language proficiency levels, providing tailored vocabulary lists, prompts, sentence frames, and language practices relevant to the STEAM content being taught. These supports help MLs learn new terms and phrases within the context of their STEAM projects, making the learning process more relevant and effective. Moreover, AI systems can provide multimodal support, accommodating to different learning styles. For instance, AI-driven speech recognition can convert spoken language into text, aiding students who might be more comfortable expressing their questions or thoughts verbally. Speech synthesis technologies can read out texts in multiple languages, assisting students with reading difficulties or those still mastering the language.

In terms of contextualization for community-based STEAM unit development, AI plays a crucial role in making learning culturally relevant and localized. AI can assist in designing STEAM units that incorporate culturally relevant examples and case studies, making the content more relatable for MLs. For instance, Ms. Nowak prompted ChatGPT to curate a list of local nurseries and plants. By analyzing community data, AI can help develop projects and programs that reflect local issues, encouraging students to apply their STEAM knowledge to real-world challenges in their immediate environment (e.g., Monarch Waystations, https://www.monarchwatch.org/waystations/). This contextualization helps students see the practical applications of STEAM concepts in their own communities.

Furthermore, AI can analyze student performance and engagement data to create adaptive learning pathways that cater to the unique needs of MLs. The AI adaptations include but are not limited to monarch butterfly migration data and observation resources, instructions and passages at different reading levels and in different languages, and ideas for community-based projects. These adaptive pathways allow students to progress through STEAM units at their own pace while working on meaningful and contextually relevant tasks.

Finally, AI also facilitates collaboration among students, teachers, and community members through intelligent platforms that support multilingual communication. These platforms can automatically translate messages, documents, and provides project updates, fostering inclusive participation and ensuring that all voices are heard in community-based projects. An example is that Ms. Nowak used Magic School AI to generate letters in different languages for multilingual families. Moreover, AI can recommend resources, tools, and materials best suited to the linguistic and educational needs of MLs, such as bilingual dictionaries, language learning apps, and culturally relevant STEAM resources. By optimizing resource allocation, AI ensures that MLs have access to the tools they need to succeed in STEAM education, thus reducing disparities and promoting equity.

These benefits with AI can significantly enhance the learning experience and outcomes for students from diverse linguistic backgrounds (Almelhes, 2023; Huang et al., 2023; Pokrivcakova, 2019).

Limitations of AI Tools

While AI tools are powerful in their ability to complete certain tasks, such as curating STEAM resources and providing tailored support for students with varied needs, they have several limitations, particularly in the context of teaching and learning with MLs. One significant limitation is the lack of linguistic diversity (Kiaer, 2023). NLPs like ChatGPT do not have equal access to linguistic databases during training. Moreover, their training data are not continuously updated, so their knowledge may not reflect the most current information. Consequently, AI tools tend to perform better in European languages compared to non-European languages, particularly Asian languages with complex writing systems (Kiaer, 2023). Similarly, a study by Hendy et al. (2023) shows that the translation quality of GPT models varies between high-resource and low-resource languages, with higher quality for high-resource languages. This disparity leads Kiaer (2023) to caution that tools like ChatGPT could further reinforce the global dominance of English and other European languages. When teachers work with MLs with non-European language backgrounds, Hendy et al. (2023) suggest cross-checking the GPT translation with other translation systems to enhance the translation quality. Additionally, linguistic diversity can be limited in NLPs because newly emerging vocabulary or expressions developed after their training period may not be included in their knowledge base.

Another limitation concerns pragmatic diversity, which is the ability to understand the nuanced variations in human languages across different social and cultural contexts for various communicative purposes (Kiaer, 2023). This implies that overreliance on AI tools might not be sufficient to address the diverse linguistic and cultural backgrounds of MLs. To ensure that MLs receive appropriate and effective language instruction, it is critical for teachers to apply culturally responsive teaching strategies and provide students with opportunities for purposeful language uses in meaningful social contexts.

Further, a critical limitation of AI tools in processing language is their limited ability to operate in multiple languages simultaneously. This is significantly different from how multilinguals naturally communicate, often engaging in translanguaging, where they fluidly switch back and forth between languages for meaningful purposes. AI tools are not flexible in processing coexisting linguistic codes from different languages at the same time, nor can they fully support MLs in utilizing all their linguistic resources to convey meaning. As a result, there is still a long way to go before AI tools can be trained to think and communicate like a multilingual individual.

Finally, additional concerns about AI include (1) the AI's focus on addressing the students' needs using the "deficit model" embedded in the algorithm; (2) potential bias and fairness in assessment designed by AI; and (3) building on students' strengths while protecting their privacy (Cardona et al., 2023). As technology evolves rapidly, teachers need more time and support to develop effective strategies to address these concerns.

Conclusion

This chapter emphasizes the importance of equipping STEAM teachers with the tools and strategies needed to thoughtfully integrate technology, enhancing the learning experiences of MLs. Grounded in Ms. Nowak's class in a rural community context, we explored the alignment of ISTE and TESOL technology standards, and three technology frameworks, with WIDA. Based on this knowledge, we presented a practical evaluation checklist to guide educators' decisions on selecting and using technology with MLs. By examining the Seesaw app, we demonstrated how collaborative and adaptive learning activities, enacting the principles of the ESEM Framework in meaningful ways, can engage and empower MLs and their families.

Recognizing the rapid advancements in technology, we also delved into the potentials and challenges posed by AI in STEAM education and highlighted its implications for teaching and learning. This work serves as a call to action for educators to embrace innovative tools while maintaining a critical focus on inclusivity, adaptability, and the unique needs of MLs, ultimately fostering a more equitable and enriching learning environment.

References

Adefris, T. (2024). *Butterfly: The life cycle of the painted lady* (Bilingual Ed.). Little Monarch Press.

Almelhes, S. (2023). A review of artificial intelligence adoption in second-language learning. *Theory and Practice in Language Studies, 13*(5), 1259–1269. https://doi.org/10.17507/tpls.1305.21

Cardona, M. A., Rodríguez, R. J., & Ishmael, K. (2023). *Artificial intelligence and future of teaching and learning: Insights and recommendations.* U.S. Department of Education, Office of Educational Technology. https://www.ed.gov/sites/ed/files/documents/ai-report/ai-report.pdf

Fairbairn, S., & Jones-Vo, S. (2010). *Differentiating instruction and assessment for English language learners: A guide for K-12 teachers.* Caslon.

Gundersheimer, B. (2019). *Señorita mariposa* (Bilingual Ed.). Neal Porter Books.

Hendy, A., Abdelrehim, M., Sharaf, A., Raunak, V., Gabr, M., Matsushita, H., Kim, Y. J., Afify, M., & Awadalla, H. H. (2023). *How good are GPT models at machine translation? A comprehensive evaluation.* Microsoft. https://arxiv.org/pdf/2302.09210

How, M., & Hung, W. (2019). Educing AI-thinking in science, technology, engineering, arts, and mathematics (STEAM) education. *Education Sciences, 9*(3), 184. https://doi.org/10.3390/EDUCSCI9030184

Huang, X., Zou, D., Cheng, G., Chen, X., & Xie, H. (2023). Trends, research issues and applications of artificial intelligence in language education. *Educational Technology & Society, 26*(1), 112–131.

Huynh, T., & Gonzalez, V. (2024). AI for reading and writing in ELT at the primary and secondary levels. *TESOL Blog.* https://www.tesol.org/blog/

posts/ai-for-reading-and-writing-in-elt-at-the-primary-and-secondary-levels/

International Society for Technology in Education (ISTE). (2024). *Standards.* https://www.iste.org/standards

Kiaer, J. (2023). *A linguist's response to the recent release of ChatGPT.* https://issuu.com/kiaerjieun/docs/alongside_ai1-2/s/18686108

Kolb, L. (2019). *Triple E framework.* https://www.tripleeframework.com

Madison, A. (2012). *Velma Gratch and the way cool butterfly.* Dragonfly Books.

Mishra, P., & Koehler, M. J. (2006). Technological pedagogical content knowledge: A framework for teacher knowledge. *Teachers College Record, 108*(6), 1017–1054. https://journals.sagepub.com/doi/pdf/10.1111/j.1467-9620.2006.00684.x

Muhisn, Z., Ahmad, M., Omar, M., & Muhisn, S. (2019). The impact of socialization on collaborative learning method in e-Learning Management System (eLMS). *International Journal of Emerging Technologies in Learning, 14*(20), 137–148.

Pokrivcakova, S. (2019). Preparing teachers for the application of AI-powered technologies in foreign language education. *Journal of Language and Cultural Education, 7*(3), 135–153.

Puentedura, R. R. (2013). *SAMR model substitution, augmentation, modification, redefinition.* https://d1pf6s1cgoc6y0.cloudfront.net/5fdcf2f7 3b804107b4fa3f2b6177affa.pdf

Romo-Rabago, M., & Torres, L. (n.d.). *Lotli the monarch butterfly* (Bilingual Ed.). Monarch Joint Venture.

Ruiz, P., & Fusco, J. (n.d.). *Glossary of artificial intelligence terms for educators.* Center for Integrative Research in Computing and Learning Sciences. https://circls.org/educatorcircls/ai-glossary

Tang, K. Y., Chang, C. Y., & Hwang, G. J. (2023). Trends in artificial intelligence-supported e-learning: A systematic review and co-citation network analysis (1998–2019). *Interactive Learning Environments, 31*(4), 2134–2152.

TESOL International Association. (2008). *TESOL technology standards framework.* https://www.call-is.org/WP/wp-content/uploads/2023/06/TESOL-Technology-Standards-Framework-Open-2023.pdf

TESOL Writing Team. (2018). *The 6 principles for exemplary teaching of English learners.* TESOL Press.

Tour, E. (2020). Teaching digital literacies in EAL/ESL classrooms: Practical strategies. *TESOL Journal, 11*(1), 1–12.

WIDA. (2014). *Focus on technology in the classroom.* https://wida.wisc.edu/sites/default/files/resource/FocusOn-Technology-in-the-Classroom.pdf

WIDA. (2020). *English language development (ELD) standards framework, 2020 edition: Kindergarten-grade 12.* Board of the University of Wisconsin System. https://wida.wisc.edu/teach/standards/eld

Xu, W., & Ouyang, F. (2022). The application of AI technologies in STEM education: A systematic review from 2011 to 2021. *International Journal of STEM Education, 9,* 59. https://doi.org/10.1186/s40594-022-00377-5

Ziegler, N., & González-Lloret, M. (2022). *The Routledge handbook of second language acquisition and technology.* Routledge.

8

STEAM Teacher Professional Development, Collaboration, and Advocacy

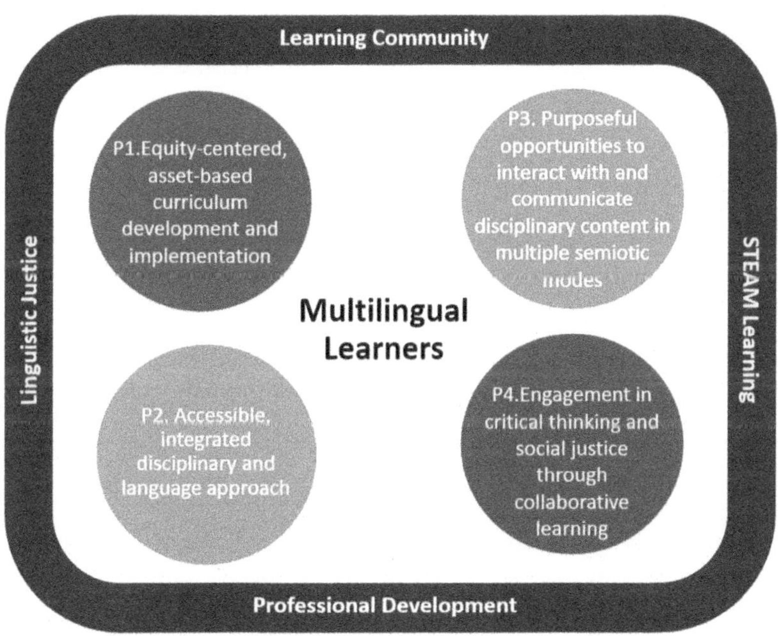

Figure 8.1 ESEM Framework

Table 8.1 Focused Core Principles and Key Practices in ESEM Framework

Focused Core Principles	Key Teaching Practices
P1. Equity-centered, asset-based curriculum development and implementation	P1.1 Ensure that curriculum content is relevant, inclusive, and accessible to all students. P1.2 Design learning units that are informed by standards and critical issues in the local and global communities. P1.3 Develop learning experiences that reflect and build on the cultural and linguistic assets of MLs and diverse disciplinary practices. P1.4 Provide opportunities for MLs to see themselves reflected positively in the curriculum and learning environment. P1.5 Implement teaching strategies that recognize and value MLs' linguistic and cultural assets.
P4. Engagement in critical thinking and social justice through collaborative learning	P4.1 Foster a classroom culture that respects each other, values critical thinking, and builds community. P4.2 Encourage MLs to critically examine issues of power, privilege, and inequality in a disciplinary context. P4.3 Facilitate collaborative learning experiences that promote critical inquiry, evaluate multiple perspectives, and build empathy. P4.4 Provide opportunities for MLs to generate evidence-based arguments on social justice topics, drawing on their diverse cultural perspectives and experiences. P4.5 Encourage MLs to take action on social justice issues that have impact on their communities, promoting agency and advocacy.

This chapter explores three interconnected topics: teacher professional development (PD), collaboration, and advocacy. We begin by discussing the importance of teacher PD, including the reasons and methods for participation. This is further illustrated by showing how insights gained from PD can be applied to enhance STEAM teaching and learning for MLs. We then discuss the topic of collaboration, emphasizing how the collaborative efforts of two teachers can significantly impact both MLs' learning outcomes and teacher growth. Finally, we delve into the concept of advocacy in the context of supporting MLs in STEAM, identifying specific action steps educators can take for effective ML advocacy. Class Profile 2

Table 8.2 Class Profile 2

Context	Suburban, 3rd grade, ESL pull-out and push-in model
Teachers	**Mr. Gilbert** (a monolingual English classroom teacher) and **Ms. Fang** (a bilingual Chinese/English ESL teacher)

Selected ML Profiles	**Olha**
	• Born in Ukraine but moved with her family to the US six months ago. Olha is considered a newcomer.
	• **Ukrainian**
	  ○ Oracy: expanding
	  ○ Literacy: developing
	• **English**
	  ○ Oracy: emerging
	  ○ Literacy: entering
	
	Lin
	• Born in Australia to Chinese parents and moved back to China when he was five years old. The family immigrated to the US one year ago.
	• **Chinese**
	  ○ Oracy: developing
	  ○ Literacy: beginning
	• **English**
	  ○ Oracy: developing
	  ○ Literacy: emerging

(see Table 8.2) is used as the context for examining MLs' STEAM teaching and learning. Chapter 8 resources on the publisher's companion website provide additional information to support the topics in the chapter.

What's Going on with Lin?

By the end of the first trimester of the school year, Mr. Gilbert grew increasingly concerned about Lin's academic progress. During STEAM activities, for instance, Lin often seemed lost, frequently looking around for cues and hesitating to engage with the materials or participate in group discussions. When Ms. Fang, the ESL teacher who provided the push-in service twice a week, was not in the classroom, Lin remained quiet and withdrawn. To support Lin, Mr. Gilbert offered hands-on learning experiences, provided a list of key academic terms, and organized group work as accommodations. Additionally, he modified Lin's homework by reducing the amount of work required for completion. However, Lin did not consistently turn in his homework. Feeling worried and discouraged, Mr. Gilbert decided to have a conversation with Ms. Fang. They met in the teacher's lounge to discuss Lin's progress.

> Mr. Gilbert: Hello, Ms. Fang! I know you've been working with Lin in the small group setting for a few months now. How's he doing?
>
> Ms. Fang: Hi, Mr. Gilbert! Lin is doing well in my small group. He's a very smart kid with a wealth of knowledge on many topics. As long as I provide the support he needs, he's excited to learn. Lin enjoys participating in the group and loves sharing the news about his baby sister and his favorite Pokémon.
>
> Mr. Gilbert: That's good to hear! Lin seems to be a completely different kid when you're not in my room. Right now we are working on a unit on the ecosystem. Lin doesn't participate much and shows little interest in what we're doing. He often doesn't complete his homework. I'm not sure what's going on.
>
> Ms. Fang: Oh no! I'm happy to set up a time to meet with you and discuss more ways to support Lin.
>
> Mr. Gilbert: That sounds like a great plan!
>
> Ms. Fang: Absolutely! I've got some great strategies from a recent PD session I attended. I'm sure you do the same. I look forward to our meeting when we can share the takeaways from these PDs and create an action plan for Lin!

Why Do We Need to Participate in Teacher Professional Development?

In the above scenario, Mr. Gilbert and Ms. Fang were committed to enhancing MLs' learning experiences by collaboratively integrating insights from their ongoing PDs. This example elaborates the importance of PD for educators working with MLs in STEAM education. PD promotes equity by equipping teachers with the latest strategies and methodologies, helping bridge the achievement gap, and ensuring culturally relevant teaching practices (Darling-Hammond et al., 2017a). It also leads to improved student outcomes as teachers become adept at fostering critical thinking, creativity, and problem-solving skills among MLs (Desimone & Garet, 2015). Moreover, as education evolves, ongoing professional development keeps teachers up-to-date with new educational technologies, pedagogical theories, and advancements in STEAM (Herro & Quigley, 2017).

Here are some common questions related to participating in continuous PD. One frequently asked question is how to find PD opportunities that are the most valuable for one's professional growth. To address this question, we encourage educators to become members of community groups and professional organizations, as these typically organize regular workshops and conferences. For instance, the National Science Teaching Association (NSTA) is a national organization for science educators and professionals who are dedicated to developing and implementing best practices in teaching science and STEM. Similarly, Teaching English to Speakers of Other Languages (TESOL) is an international organization that provides PDs and resources from a community of passionate educators and researchers committed to enhancing English language teaching.

Another common concern related to PD is how to fund these opportunities. The answer to the question varies. In some cases, school districts have available resources and can invite experts for in-house training. In other instances, schools may have available funding for educators to attend PD opportunities outside of the district. For those working in underfunded districts with limited resources, securing grants or funding can provide access to high-quality PD programs focused on STEAM education for MLs. Please refer to the Chapter 8 resources on the publisher's companion website for more information about grants.

Additionally, with the advancement of technology, there are many online resources, such as webinars, MOOCs (massive open online courses), and online professional learning communities available free of charge, offering accessible and flexible opportunities for professional growth (Trust & Horrocks, 2017). For a list of professional organizations, STEAM web resources, and PD funding opportunities, refer to the Chapter 8 resources on the publisher's companion website.

In the following, we will explore how Mr. Gilbert and Ms. Fang engaged in different PD opportunities and how the insights gained from these sessions transformed STEAM teaching and learning for MLs.

STEAM-Focused PD for Mr. Gilbert— Experiential Learning

Mr. Gilbert constantly sought ways to engage his students in experiential learning through hands-on, real-world STEAM activities. Recognizing the increasing significance of STEAM education, he eagerly enrolled in a weeklong summer PD program focused on integrating experiential learning into earthquake science education. This PD, offered by the Smithsonian Science Education Center, enhanced Mr. Gilbert's understanding of seismic activity, tectonic plates, and the impact of earthquakes on communities, while also providing strategies for making complex scientific concepts accessible to elementary students through experiential learning.

Mr. Gilbert took part in interactive sessions where he learned how to incorporate students' real-world experience into the earthquake unit, utilize classroom materials and visuals to help students interpret earthquake data, and develop cross-curricular activities that integrated math, geography, and language arts. The hands-on nature of the training boosted his confidence in designing engaging STEAM units for all of his students. As the new school year began, Mr. Gilbert was ready to incorporate his PD learnings into his STEAM unit.

Language-Focused PD for Ms. Fang— Translanguaging in STEAM Education

Early in the school year, Ms. Fang had the opportunity to participate in the multilingual conference organized by the state education resource center. One of the sessions she attended was on supporting MLs in STEAM learning through translanguaging. The concept of translanguaging was introduced in Chapter 2. A quick review of translanguaging theory suggests that learners utilize a range of linguistic and nonlinguistic resources to construct and communicate meaning (García, 2009; Hua et al., 2019; Li, 2018; Sherris & Adami, 2019). In addition to deepening her understanding of translanguaging as an equity-focused pedagogy, the PD session equipped Ms. Fang with practical strategies for supporting MLs' to engage in key science and engineering practices (NGSS Lead States, 2013). Further, an important takeaway was that translanguaging benefits all students and that monolingual teachers can create space for it in their classrooms (Pierson et al., 2021). Ms. Fang synthesized translanguaging strategies from the PD session (Andersen et al., 2022; Pierson et al., 2021) in Table 8.3 to provide an easy reference for sharing with other teachers.

Table 8.3 Translanguaging Strategies for STEAM Education

Translanguaging Strategies	Examples	Sample Teacher Actions	Sample Student Activities
Establishing rationale for translanguaging in STEAM	Infographics, bilingual children's books, interactive websites, and multimedia presentations	• Selecting model texts that use a variety of modes for communication • Modeling how different linguistic and nonlinguistic modes are used for specific audiences and purposes	• Engaging in discussions to identify modes of communication and their purposes • Reflecting on the effectiveness of model texts' use of linguistic and nonlinguistic modes of communication
Leveraging students' full linguistic and nonlinguistic repertoire	*Linguistic repertoire*: Primary language(s), everyday language, emerging English, academic STEAM language, and structural forms (e.g., CER) typical of language in STEAM *Nonlinguistic repertoire*: Gestures, kinesthetic movements, visuals (e.g., drawings and pictures, mathematical or scientific symbols and formulas, data tables, graphs or charts, and models) and visual aids (e.g., Venn diagram or T-chart)	• Regularly demonstrate interest in and validate the diverse linguistic and cultural resources students bring to the classroom • Providing students opportunities for translanguaging (e.g., instructional materials in multiple languages, partner work with MLs, promoting multilingual and multimodal communication) • Design activities that naturally invite students to use their multilingual resources	• Working with ML peers to explore, discuss, and explain STEAM concepts using multiple languages and modalities • Communicating learning through multilingual and multimodal presentations • Reflecting on how their peers use language, gestures, and other modes to convey ideas during group activities

Implementing Insights from PD to STEAM Learning

When Mr. Gilbert and Ms. Fang met to address the concerns about Lin, they decided to collaboratively redesign an upcoming unit titled "Why Does the Earth Shake?" by integrating strategies they learned from their PD to support MLs. The unit was informed by the following standards: NGSS 3 LS4-1, 4 ESS1-1, CCSS MP2, MP4, MP5, NCAS 10. Further, earthquakes are a critical local issue for the school, which is located in the suburbs of San Francisco, California, near the San Andreas Fault—a major fault line responsible for many of the region's earthquakes. Earthquakes are also a critical global issue due to their frequent occurrence and their potential devastating impacts to communities, infrastructure, and economies.

Informed by his summer PD on experiential learning, Mr. Gilbert was determined to provide an immersive learning experience that would engage all senses of his students. He first researched the earthquake-related exhibits at the California Academy of Sciences in San Francisco. The exhibits include a state-of-the-art earthquake simulator, allowing learners to experience the sensation of a real earthquake and better understand the impact of seismic events. Moreover, the academy offered interactive shake tables where students could build and test structures to see how they would withstand various magnitudes of shaking. With these exciting opportunities in mind, Mr. Gilbert carefully planned a field trip to align with his classroom lessons and took care of all of the logistics, such as arranging the transportation, obtaining permission slips, and identifying parent volunteers. Additionally, in the redesign process, Mr. Gilbert regularly referred to the resources and strategies he had encountered during the PD, such as those provided by the National Earth Science Teachers Association (NESTA) and National Science Teaching Association (NSTA). He also used online tools and data from the United States Geological Survey (USGS) to keep the lessons relevant and up-to-date. To effectively integrate language development in content, Ms. Fang offered one-on-one time with Mr. Gilbert so that they could incorporate the translanguaging strategies in the redesign. In addition to showing the results of the redesign, we will elaborate on how the enhanced STEAM learning experiences address the ESEM Framework, specifically Core Principles 1 and 4 and the associated key teaching practices (see Table 8.1).

Table 8.4 features sample 5E instructional activities in the explore and explain stages, which were co-designed and co-taught by Mr. Gilbert

Table 8.4 Collaborative Implementation of PD in the STEAM Teaching and Learning

Sample Instructional Activities in Explore and Explain Stages	Enacted Sample Core Principles and Key Teaching Practices
<ul><li>With support from Ms. Fang, Mr. Gilbert provided a variety of multilingual and multimodal resources for students to research different aspects of earthquakes, including the causes of earthquakes, the history of significant earthquakes in California, how buildings were designed to be earthquake resistant, and the science behind earthquake detection and measurement. Equipped with these resources, students worked in small groups to investigate and construct claims about the causes of earthquakes. The academic vocabulary, such as *tectonic plates*, *fault lines*, and *seismic waves*, were naturally introduced and practiced as students were engaged in doing the investigation.</li><li>MLs were paired with other multilingual peers who could help them understand specific words and phrases. In Lin's case (the only Chinese-language speaker in the room), Ms. Fang remained with his group to offer assistance in translating between Chinese and English as needed.</li><li>Using the provided CER (claim, evidence, and reasoning) graphic organizer, students constructed their claims using either languages or a combination of gestures, drawings, and writing. Their claims addressed various aspects of earthquake causes, such as tectonic plate movements, volcanic activity, or human-induced factors.</li><li>In small groups, students worked on creating a simple 3D model of tectonic plates using foam sheets and other commonly available classroom materials to demonstrate the evidence and reasoning that supported their claims. By sliding, colliding, and separating the foam pieces, the students were able to visualize how these movements could lead to earthquakes, helping to deepen their understanding of the concept.</li></ul>	P1.1 Ensure that curriculum content is relevant, inclusive, and accessible to all students. P1.3 Develop learning experiences that reflect and build on the cultural and linguistic assets of MLs and diverse disciplinary practices. P1.5 Implement teaching strategies that recognize and value MLs' linguistic and cultural assets. P4.3 Facilitate collaborative learning experiences that promote critical inquiry, evaluate multiple perspectives, and build empathy. P4.4 Provide opportunities for MLs to generate evidence-based arguments on social justice topics, drawing on their diverse cultural perspectives and experiences.

Table 8.4 (*Continued*)

Sample Instructional Activities in Explore and Explain Stages	Enacted Sample Core Principles and Key Teaching Practices
• Throughout the process, students engaged in discussions and negotiations about the model design, using different languages (e.g., everyday language, academic language, and home language) and multimodal resources such as gestures, body movement, or drawings. • Upon completing their models, students presented them to the class. Tapping into multilingual and multimodal resources, all students were able to contribute to the presentations. They provided reasoning and used evidence from their research and model to support their claims. • For the whole class, Ms. Fang summarized the various ways students constructed their explanations, integrating the discipline-specific CER language structure into students' linguistic repertoire. Students in small groups continued to research one aspect of earthquakes and prepare a presentation. • On the next day, Mr. Gilbert showed the class a local map and a data chart of earthquake magnitude, energy release, and shaking intensity (e.g., https://www.usgs.gov/media/images/eq-magnitude-energy-release-and-shaking-intensity-6) and encouraged students to ask questions. Ms. Fang modeled a few questions and reinforced that questions could be shared in any modality, whether through acting, speaking, or writing. One question that many students asked was how the shaking intensity of an earthquake is measured. • To help students answer the question, Mr. Gilbert introduced the class to seismographs and their role in detecting and recording earthquake activity. He guided the students in constructing basic seismographs using cardboard, string, and markers. • Engaging in simulated practices like those of STEM professionals, the students experimented with their seismographs, shaking the table to simulate an earthquake and observing how the markers recorded the vibrations on paper. This activity not only reinforced their understanding of seismic waves but also sparked excitement and curiosity about the technology used to study earthquakes.	

and Ms. Fang. The companion website provides activities for full 5E instructional stages. The activities center on engaging MLs in one of the key science and engineering practices defined by the NGSS Lead States (2013): constructing explanations. Table 8.4 also illustrates how these activities enact sample core principles and key teaching practices from the ESEM Framework.

Why Do We Need to Collaborate?

In the previous section, we showed how participating in continuous PD helps educators stay current with best practices and makes a positive impact on student learning. What made the redesign and implementation of STEAM teaching truly transformative in the third-grade classroom was the collaboration between Mr. Gilbert and Ms. Fang. This underscores the critical importance of collaboration in effectively serving MLs.

While collaboration between families, schools, and various community partners is essential, this chapter primarily focuses on collaboration among educators within the school setting. The partnership between schools and families is explored in detail in Chapter 6. As the above example illustrates, MLs excel when content and language teachers adopt a highly integrated and collaborative approach to designing and implementing a rich curriculum with high expectations. This approach engages students in developing language skills while simultaneously learning content knowledge. Collaboration not only boosts student academic performance (Greenberg Motamedi et al., 2019) but also fosters teacher learning (Darling-Hammond et al., 2017b). Below we will review each teacher's key takeaways from this collaboration.

By collaborating with Ms. Fang, Mr. Gilbert, a monolingual English-speaking teacher, successfully integrated experiential learning and translanguaging pedagogy into STEAM teaching. He also strengthened culturally responsive teaching by designing learning activities that drew on and expanded MLs' rich life experiences and cultural assets. Mr. Gilbert recognized and embraced his dual identity as both a STEAM teacher and a language teacher.

Meanwhile, Ms. Fang, an English as a second language teacher, underwent a transformation in her professional identity. Recognizing her own bilingualism in Chinese and English as linguistic assets, she shifted her focus from solely teaching English to embracing multiple languages and literacies. This allowed her to draw on her own linguistic assets to better support Lin, a bilingual Chinese and English learner. Further, the collaboration deepened Ms. Fang's understanding of STEAM content through her collaboration with Mr. Gilbert. This experience equipped her with the knowledge and skills to better serve MLs by developing an integrated ESL curriculum that connects their mainstream classroom learning to pull-out settings.

Further, Breshears (2004) describes the status and working conditions of language support staff as "the lowest of the low" professions. Investigating the high attrition rate of ESL teachers, especially those from culturally and linguistically diverse backgrounds, Wong (2022) identified several contributing factors, including unsupportive colleagues and the marginalized status of MLs and ESL teachers. In reality, ESL teachers are often hired on a part-time basis due to fluctuating ML numbers and funding constraints. Even when employed full-time, they frequently have to travel between schools to fulfill their workload. Limited space in schools often relegates ESL pull-out groups to instruction in storage rooms or basements. However, the success of the collaboration significantly elevated Ms. Fang's status as a language support specialist among her colleagues. With newfound respect from her peers, Ms. Fang gained the confidence to embrace future collaborations with other content area teachers.

What Does Collaboration with Educators Look Like?

To initiate and sustain collaboration, educators have various models to consider. A collaboration cycle proposed by WIDA (2020) includes four key components: co-planning, co-teaching, co-assessing, and co-reflecting. Below we will describe each component and provide examples for elaboration.

Co-planning: Co-planning is the cornerstone of successful collaboration. Dedicated co-planning time for content and ESL teachers offers valuable opportunities to identify the challenges MLs face and strategically allocate resources to address those challenges. A critical step of co-planning is to identify the most prominent key language uses (WIDA, 2020) necessary to meet content objectives. In the scenario discussed in this chapter, Mr. Gilbert and Ms. Fang intentionally scheduled time to meet and discuss how to integrate experiential learning and translanguaging strategies to support MLs like Lin to construct explanations (key language use: explain).

Co-teaching: Co-teaching helps to dismantle the traditional divide between content and ESL teachers and embrace the notion that all teachers are language teachers (TESOL Writing Team, 2018). Through co-teaching, we also model for all students how languages are used to achieve various functions in disciplines. There are several co-teaching models with specific group configurations and clearly defined roles and responsibilities for each educator (Friend & Cook, 1996). We explain the collaborative teaching models for MLs in Table 8.5 based on the recommendation of Honigsfeld and Dove (2019).

The co-teaching model used by Mr. Gilbert and Ms. Fang is "One Leads, One Teaches on Purpose." This means that Mr. Gilbert led the lesson while Ms. Fang co-taught to purposefully build on MLs' strengths and support their needs. Consulting with all the partners can help schools select the model that best fits their context.

Co-assessing: Valid and reliable assessment tools are essential for gathering valuable data on students' growth and areas of need. However, when MLs are assessed on content learning objectives without considering their language needs, the data may lack validity. Co-assessment involves content and ESL teachers working together to design and implement assessments that address both content and language learning objectives. WIDA (2020) offers a variety of tools that guide teachers to assess MLs' English language development across all four language domains (i.e., speaking, listening, reading, and writing).

Co-reflecting: Co-reflection involves two key aspects: reflecting on what we have learned about our MLs and what we have learned about ourselves as educators. Reflecting on the former based on formative and summative data can provide insights into MLs' linguistic and cultural assets, enriching their profiles as learners and documenting their growth. Reflecting on the latter allows teachers to assess their own learning and identify areas for further professional development. This process not only enhances instructional practices but also fosters a continuous cycle of improvement and growth for both teachers and students.

Table 8.5 Collaborative Teaching Models for MLs

Student Group	Model	Diagram	Description
One Large Group	One Leads, One Teaches on Purpose	T S S S S S S S S S S S T S S S S S	One teacher leads the lesson while the other provides targeted support to one or more students to achieve specific learning targets.
	Two Teach Same Content	T T S S S S S S S S S S S S S S S S S S	Both teachers co-teach the lesson and offer all students the chance to engage with content and develop skills.
	One Teachers, One Assesses	T S S S S S S S S S S S S ↗T S S S S S S	One teacher teaches the lesson while the other gathers specific formative assessment data.
Two Groups	Two Teachers Teach the Same Content	T T S S S S S S S S S S S S S S S S S S	Each group is led by a teacher focusing on the same learning targets but utilizing different methods, languages, or instructional approaches.
	One Teacher Preteaches, One Teaches Alternative Information	T T S S S S S S S S S S S S S S S S S S	One group focuses on developing foundational skills or building background knowledge while the other engages in enrichment or extension activities.
	One Teacher Reteaches, One Teaches Alternative Information	T T S S S S S S S S S S S S S S S S S S	One group focuses on review and practice activities while the other engages in enrichment or extension activities.

Adapted from Honigsfeld & Dove (2019).

What Is Advocacy? Why and How Do We Advocate for MLs?

While continuously engaging in PD and collaborating with colleagues are essential in the education profession, a critical role that educators play is advocating for students. Advocacy in different contexts has various meanings. In the context of working with MLs, it refers to educators actively supporting and promoting MLs' rights, needs, and opportunities both within and beyond the educational system. Despite the rapidly increasing population of MLs nationwide, they remain underserved and underrepresented in the public education system, largely due to a lack of highly qualified educators, resources, and access to a rigorous curriculum (NEA, 2015).

The majority of the MLs are from the BIPOC (Black, Indigenous, and people of color) communities (NCES, 2024). These students often encounter barriers, such as limited access to high-quality education, mentorship, and resources, that can impede their progress in STEAM disciplines (McGee & Bentley, 2017). The inclusion of BIPOC students in STEAM is critical given the historical and ongoing underrepresentation of these groups in these fields. It is, therefore, important to advocate for the creation of an inclusive learning environment, along with culturally responsive curricula that reflect the diverse experiences and histories of BIPOC students. Such curricula can help students see themselves in the content they are learning, thereby increasing engagement and persistence in STEAM fields.

Further, while Asian American and Pacific Islanders (AAPI) are part of the BIPOC group, it is crucial to address the unique challenges faced by AAPI students. A common social discourse regarding AAPI groups is that they are stereotypically perceived as high achieving. This broad generalization overlooks significant disparities within the community. For instance, Southeast Asian and Pacific Islander groups such as Hmong often face disadvantages due to this stereotype. Despite being categorized under the broad Asian American label, these groups encounter educational challenges, including poverty, limited access to academic resources, and cultural barriers that impede their success in STEM (Museus, 2014). Ironically, these students are frequently excluded from programs designed to support underrepresented groups in STEAM, based on the misconception that all Asian Americans are overrepresented in these fields. This oversight perpetuates systemic inequalities and hinders the success of all students in these vital disciplines. We need thoughtful consideration to advocate effectively for the AAPI community within the context of STEAM. It is essential to fostering a sense of community and belonging for all students.

Confronted with situations where MLs are denied opportunities to reach their full academic potential, educators have the responsibility to ensure that MLs' voices are heard and their needs are met. The National Education Association (NEA) (2015) emphasizes that "at its core, advocacy is about action" (p. 10). This means that educators actively advocate for issues impacting MLs and work to promote equity and justice. For example, creating spaces where ML students feel valued and supported can encourage collaboration and peer support, which are important for academic and professional success. When students see themselves reflected in the community around them, they are more likely to persist and thrive in their STEAM pursuits. Moreover, the most powerful and impactful advocacy for MLs is achieved through collective collaboration (NEA, 2015).

What are the specific action steps educators can take for effective ML advocacy? NEA (2015) outlines five steps. We use the third-grade class profile introduced at the beginning of the chapter to elaborate on each of the five advocacy action steps. With a successful co-teaching model piloted by Mr. Gilbert and Ms. Fang, MLs such as Lin and Olha made significant achievements in content and language learning. Mr. Gilbert and Ms. Fang were on a mission to advocate for the school district to move from the pull-out/push-in model to the co-teaching model to ensure MLs' access to rigorous curriculum while addressing their language rights and needs.

Step 1: Isolate the issue. Mr. Gilbert noticed that Lin was not engaged in class. However, Ms. Fang, the ESL teacher, had very limited time in providing push-in service for Lin.

Step 2: Identify your allies. Mr. Gilbert and Ms. Fang communicated with other general education teachers and found that they were also concerned about the academic progress of MLs due to the lack of consistent and structured language support in the mainstream class. Together, they formed allies to investigate the issue further and identify solutions.

Step 3: Be clear on the rights of MLs. Mr. Gilbert and Ms. Fang organized a professional learning community (PLC) with one representative general educator from each grade level to evaluate the strengths and weaknesses of various language program models, in accordance with regulations set by the state board of education. They also compared the impact of co-teaching on MLs' content and language development to that of the pull-out/push-in model, drawing on relevant research. Based on their findings, they created an action plan that highlighted staff PD on co-teaching and designated release time for educators to collaborate.

Step 4: Organize and educate others. Mr. Gilbert and Ms. Fang arranged a meeting with school administrators to share their action plan. With the support from the school principal, they shared the learning from the PLC and the action plan at a staff meeting, inviting feedback from the entire school community.

Step 5: Identify your outlets for change. Mr. Gilbert, Ms. Fang, and their colleagues recognized that the change to co-teaching required support from both the district and state levels. They shared their advocacy plan at viable outlets, such as district-wide PD forums, school board meetings, and state bilingual conferences.

Conclusion

This chapter uses a third-grade classroom vignette to explore a comprehensive approach to advancing equity and social justice for MLs through the triad of teacher PD, collaboration, and advocacy. Continuous PD provides educators with research-based strategies for effective STEAM and languaging practices. The impact of PD on MLs is amplified when coupled with collaboration among educators, as elaborated by the example of Mr. Gilbert, the classroom teacher, and Ms. Fang, the language specialist. Moreover, a strong focus on advocacy enables educators to actively support and address MLs' specific needs and create action plans for changes. Through PD, collaboration, and advocacy, educators play a pivotal role in creating an inclusive, equitable, and empowering educational landscape for MLs, especially within STEAM disciplines. The companion website provides additional resources related to topics in this chapter.

References

Andersen, S., Pérez, K. M., & González-Howard, M. (2022). Reimagining science lessons through translanguaging: Supporting multilingual students' scientific sensemaking in the context of science and engineering practices. *Science Scope, 46*(2), 25–31.

Breshears, S. (2004). Professionalization and exclusion in ESL teaching. *TESL Canada Journal Revue, 4*(Special Issue), 23–39. https://files.eric.ed.gov/fulltext/EJ847921.pdf

Darling-Hammond, L., Hyler, M. E., & Gardner, M. (2017a). *Effective teacher professional development.* Learning Policy Institute. https://learningpolicyinstitute.org/sites/default/files/product-files/Effective_Teacher_Professional_Development_REPORT.pdf

Darling-Hammond, L., Campbell, C., Goodwin, A. L., Hammerness, K., Low, E. L., McIntyre, A., Sato, M., & Zeichner, K. (2017b). *Empowered educators: How high-performing systems shape teaching quality around the world.* John Wiley & Sons.

Desimone, L. M., & Garet, M. S. (2015). Best practices in teacher's professional development in the United States. *Psychology, Society, & Education, 7*(3), 252–263.

Friend, M., & Cook, L. (1996). *Interactions: Collaboration skills for school professionals.* Longman.

García, O. (2009). Emergent bilinguals and TESOL: What's in a name? *TESOL Quarterly, 43*(2), 322–326.

Greenberg Motamedi, J., Vazquez, M., Gandhi, E. V., & Holmgren, M. (2019). *Beaverton School District English language development minutes, models, and outcomes.* Education Northwest.

Herro, D., & Quigley, C. (2017). Exploring teachers' perceptions of STEAM teaching through professional development: Implications for teacher educators. *Professional Development in Education, 43,* 416–438. https://doi.org/10.1080/19415257.2016.1205507

Honigsfeld, A., & Dove, M. G. (2019). *Collaborating for English learners: A foundational guide to integrated practices.* Corwin Press.

Hua, Z., Li, W., & Jankowicz-Pytel, D. (2019). Translanguaging and embodied teaching and learning: Lessons from a multilingual karate club in London. *International Journal of Bilingual Education and Bilingualism, 23*(1), 65–80.

Li, W. (2018). Translanguaging as a practical theory of language. *Applied Linguistics, 39*(1), 9–30.

McGee, E. O., & Bentley, L. (2017). The equity ethic: Black and Latinx college students reengineering their STEM careers toward justice. *American Journal of Education, 123*(3), 305–339.

Museus, S. D. (2014). The culturally engaging campus environments (CECE) model: A new theory of success among racially diverse college student populations. In M. B. Paulsen (Ed.), *Higher education: Handbook of theory and research* (pp. 189–227). Springer.

National Center for Education Statistics (NCES). (2024). *English learners in public schools.* https://nces.ed.gov/programs/coe/indicator/cgf/english-learners

National Education Association. (2015). *How educators can advocate for English language learners.* https://www.colorincolorado.org/sites/default/files/ELL_AdvocacyGuide2015.pdf

NGSS Lead States. (2013). *Next Generation Science Standards: For states, by states.* National Academies Press.

Pierson, A. E., Clark, D. B., & Brady, C. E. (2021). Scientific modeling and translanguaging: A multilingual and multimodal approach to support science learning and engagement. *Science Education, 105,* 776–813. DOI:10.1002/sce.21622

Sherris, A., & Adami, E. (Eds.). (2019). *Making signs, translanguaging ethnographies: Exploring urban, rural and educational space.* Multilingual Matters.

TESOL Writing Team. (2018). *The 6 principles for exemplary teaching of English learners.* TESOL Press.

Trust, T., & Horrocks, B. (2017). "I never feel alone in my classroom": Teacher professional growth within a blended community of practice. *Professional Development in Education, 43*(4), 645–665.

WIDA Focus Bulletin. (2020). *Collaboration: Working together to serve multilingual learners.* https://wida.wisc.edu/sites/default/files/resource/FocusBulletin-Collaboration.pdf

Wong, C. Y. (2022). "ESL teachers are looked down upon": Understanding the lived experience of a first-year ESL teacher with a culturally and linguistically diverse background. *Journal of Educational Research and Practice, 12*(1), 291–303. https://eric.ed.gov/?id=EJ1373957

Part III

Conclusion

Summary of the Chapters

This book provides an in-depth exploration of how educators can enhance STEAM learning experiences for MLs through an equity-focused, culturally and linguistically responsive, and interdisciplinary approach. The centerpiece of the book is the Equitable STEAM Education for Multilingual Learners (ESEM) Framework, which is grounded in the latest research and provides a set of actionable principles and practices to guide various aspects of STEAM educators' work with MLs. Each chapter presents unique applications from the framework, emphasizing culturally relevant curriculum and instruction, linguistic justice strategies, purposeful integration of technology, family/community partnerships, and teacher professional development and collaboration to strengthen equitable STEAM learning for MLs. The following summary highlights the core contributions of each chapter.

Chapter 1 introduces the readers to MLs, moving beyond statistics to focus on individual students situated within diverse social, economic, cultural, and family contexts. It advocates for a shift from deficit-focused perspectives to an asset-based approach, where MLs' linguistic and cultural resources are celebrated as essential building blocks of STEAM learning. The chapter also advocates an integrated approach to STEAM education, emphasizing the interdisciplinary nature of contemporary problems and issues. It sets the foundation for understanding the need to design and implement STEAM education that resonate with MLs' lived experiences.

Chapter 2 introduces the ESEM Framework, which is anchored in culturally and linguistically responsive teaching, translanguaging, and critical visual literacy perspectives. This framework guides teachers in designing equitable STEAM education that bridges language and content learning, enabling MLs to build both academic skills and social agency.

The ESEM Framework emphasizes that equity in STEAM education entails both access and identity affirmation, helping students see themselves as valuable members of the STEAM community.

Chapters 3 and 4 delve into the learning community, curriculum development, implementation, and assessment strategies that make STEAM education inclusive and actionable. Educators are encouraged to create a welcoming and supportive learning community, designing project-based learning units that align with real-world issues and giving students opportunities to engage in interdisciplinary problem-solving. By centering projects on social justice topics, students can connect their STEAM learning to community needs, building a sense of agency as they propose solutions to local and global challenges.

Chapters 5 and 6 focus on designing effective STEAM instruction and developing family and community partnerships, further enriching STEAM education. Effective STEAM instruction features visual literacy and critical visual literacy strategies, student-centered inquiry, sense-making activities, community-based projects, and differentiation and ML strategies dedicated to linguistic justice. Further, reciprocal partnerships with families and community members empower educators to collaboratively design meaningful and equitable STEAM education that extends beyond the confines of the classroom. These chapters emphasize that STEAM education should be grounded in culturally relevant, multimodal instruction that honors all students' linguistic and nonlinguistic resources and fosters critical consciousness.

Chapters 7 and 8 explore technology integration and professional development as essential components for STEAM education in diverse classrooms. Technology serves as a bridge for MLs to access STEAM content in multiple languages and modalities, enhancing their understanding and engagement. Professional development initiatives and collaboration empower teachers with the skills and strategies needed to effectively integrate technology, advocate for equitable STEAM education for MLs, and adapt to the evolving landscape of education.

Revisiting the ESEM Framework

The ESEM Framework (see Figure C.1) serves as the foundation of this book, promoting equitable STEAM education for MLs by synthesizing

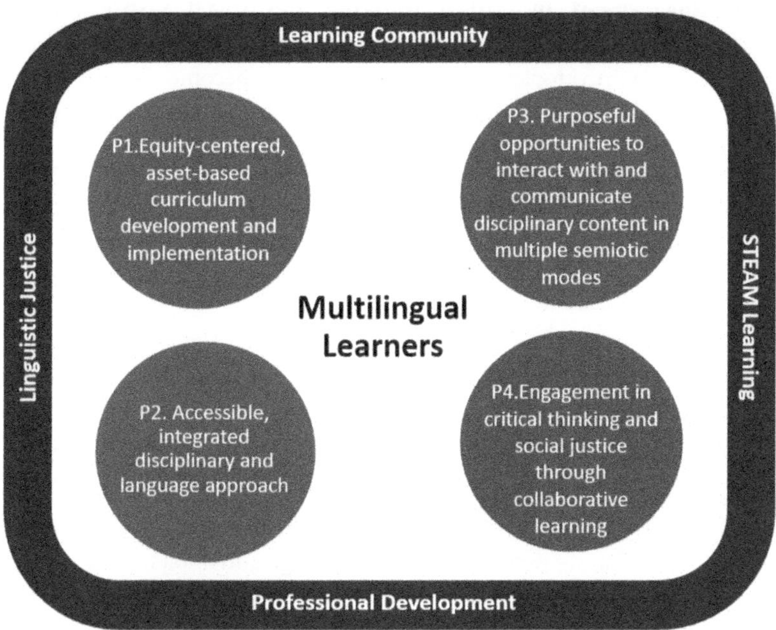

Figure C.1 The ESEM Framework

culturally and linguistically responsive teaching, translanguaging pedagogy, and critical visual literacy.

The framework consists of four core principles:

P1. **Equity-centered, asset-based curriculum development and implementation:** Teachers create inclusive content that reflects MLs' cultural and linguistic resources. By affirming students' identities within the STEAM curriculum, educators can foster a sense of belonging and empower MLs to contribute their unique perspectives to STEAM learning.

P2. **Accessible, integrated disciplinary and language approach:** This principle bridges content and language learning, allowing MLs to build STEAM proficiency through meaningful engagement in their primary languages and English.

P3. **Purposeful opportunities to interact with and communicate disciplinary content in multiple semiotic modes:** Through various communication modes (e.g., visual, oral, and written), MLs develop literacy in both language and content. Critical visual literacy is particularly important, as it empowers students to question and interpret visuals critically.

P4. Engagement in critical thinking and social justice through collaborative learning: By examining power structures and inequities within STEAM topics, MLs are encouraged to become agents of change in their communities, connecting their learning to broader social issues.

These four core principles are surrounded by different components on the four sides, each providing sociocultural, linguistic, disciplinary, and professional contexts for the core principles. Each chapter in Part II elaborates on how to enact the core principles in diverse educational settings in the ESEM Framework (see Table C.1).

- Chapter 1 introduces the rationale for an equity-focused STEAM education that values MLs' backgrounds, setting the stage for the ESEM Framework.
- Chapter 2 introduces the ESEM Framework, providing theoretical and practical guidance for its implementation.
- Chapters 3 and 4 demonstrate how to design and implement a learning community and curriculum that aligns with students' cultural contexts and emphasizes social justice, aligning with Principles 1 and 4.
- Chapters 5 and 6 apply effective strategies and develop family and community partnership, helping MLs connect their lived experiences with STEAM learning at school. These practices connect closely with all four principles.
- Chapters 7 and 8 advocate for technology integration, ongoing professional development, collaboration, and advocacy, ensuring

Table C.1 Alignment of the ESEM Framework With Chapters

Chapters	Core Principles in the ESEM Framework			
	P1	P2	P3	P4
2. ESEM Framework	X	X	X	X
3. Learning Community	X			X
4. Curriculum	X			X
5. Instruction		X	X	
6. Family and Community Partnership	X			X
7. Technology		X	X	
8. PD, Collaboration, and Advocacy	X			X

that educators are prepared to implement the ESEM Framework in a rapidly evolving, technology-driven world. These practices connect closely with all four principles.

Finally, the companion website for this book provides a plethora of additional resources such as detailed lesson plans, recommended children's book lists, STEAM-related activity resources, and PD and funding opportunities.

Looking Ahead

In a world where technology, cultural diversity, and global connectivity are constantly evolving, educators face both challenges and opportunities in designing and delivering equitable STEAM education for all students. This book serves as a guide for teachers seeking to navigate these complexities by embracing the potential of AI and digital tools while emphasizing the focus on culturally and linguistically responsive instruction. For STEAM teachers working with MLs, this book highlights the importance of seeing multilingualism as an asset, using translanguaging strategies, and fostering an inclusive learning environment that reflects students' identities. As classrooms become increasingly diverse, the need for an equity-focused approach in STEAM education will only grow. This book provides a foundation for teachers to meet these demands, equipping them with strategies and tools to build inclusive, interdisciplinary, and equity-focused STEAM curricula.

Guided by the ESEM Framework, educators can ensure that all students—not just MLs—benefit from a STEAM education that is relevant, innovative, and socially responsible. This approach enriches students' academic experiences while preparing them to thrive in an interconnected and culturally diverse world.

As Mouboua and Atobatele (2024) remind us,

Multilingual teaching approaches are essential for promoting diversity, enhancing global competence, preparing students for global careers, improving cognitive skills, and addressing equity in education. By implementing these approaches, educators can create more inclusive and effective learning environments that benefit all students, regardless of their linguistic background (p. 90).

Figure C.2 Promising STEAM Education.
Insta_photos (2021), istockphoto.com (Happy diverse school children students building robotic cars using computer).

This perspective underscores that STEAM education is not just about teaching disciplinary content but about bridging the cultural and linguistic gaps and equipping students to innovate, lead, and build a more inclusive and equitable future (see Figure C.2).

Reference

Mouboua, P. D., & Atobatele, F. A. (2024). Bridging STEM and linguistic gaps: A review of multilingual teaching approaches in science education. *Research Journal of Multidisciplinary Studies, 7*(2), 86–97. DOI:https://doi. org/10.53022/oarjms.2024.7.2.0030

Index

About the Authors

Dr. Eun Kyung Ko is an associate professor of science education at National Louis University, specializing in culturally responsive teaching and the integration of STEAM in diverse classroom settings. Her research emphasizes fostering equity and inclusion in K–12 education, focusing on strategies that support multilingual learners and underrepresented groups in STEM fields. As the co-principal investigator of the NSF-funded ENACTS (Engaging Noyce Scholars in Anti-Racist Community-Based Teaching in Biology, Chemistry, Mathematics, and Physics) project, Dr. Ko has developed professional learning sequences to empower teachers in designing inclusive STEAM learning environments that integrate computational thinking and reflect culturally sustaining pedagogies.

With a deep commitment to multicultural education, Dr. Ko's work bridges the gap between science instruction and social justice by equipping educators to address the needs of diverse student populations. Her innovative approaches, including AI-supported culturally responsive teaching tools, aim to promote justice, agency, and belonging for students from historically marginalized communities. Through her research and advocacy, Dr. Ko strives to create transformative educational experiences that prepare all students to thrive in a global, multicultural society.

Dr. Ko's research and contributions have been presented at national and international conferences, including the American Educational Research Association (AERA), the Association for Science Teacher Education (ASTE), and the International Conference on Urban Education (ICUE). Her efforts aim to prepare the next generation of educators and students to thrive in an increasingly diverse and interconnected world.

Dr. Xiaoning Chen is an associate professor and chair of the ESL/Bilingual Education Program at National Louis University. She holds a doctorate in language and literacy education from Purdue University. Dr. Chen has two decades of experience in language education and teacher training in the United States and abroad. Her research interests include visual literacy, multicultural children's literature, and multimodal literacies. She has shared her work through numerous presentations at national and international conferences, as well as publications in various journals and edited volumes. She also co-authored two volumes of *Teaching Social Studies to Multilingual Learners: Connecting Inquiry and Visual Literacy to Promote Progressive Learning* with Rowman & Littlefield, now under Bloomsbury after its acquisition. Dr. Chen has served as an International Visual Literacy Association board member since 2019 and has served two terms as an assistant editor for the *IVLA Book of the Selected Readings*. She has directed the Library of Congress Teaching With Primary Sources Regional Grant and two rounds of the STARTALK teacher training grant from the US National Security Agency.

Dr. Vishodana Thamotharan is a dedicated STEM educator and leader, serving currently as the director of STEM at National Louis University. She has served in numerous roles, including chemistry teacher, new teacher mentor, assistant professor, and managing director of a secondary STEM education program. Her work focuses on intersectional justice in education, community-based instruction, developing critically conscious educators and leaders, and the role of AI in preparing culturally responsive teachers. She is committed to fostering justice-centered educational environments.

Dr. Xiaoli Wen is the research director of the McCormick Institute for Early Childhood and a professor of early childhood education at National Louis University. She holds a PhD in human development from Purdue University. Her research centers on interventions for children from under-resourced backgrounds, including center-based preschool and home visiting programs. She has led evaluations of professional development models for early math instruction and spearheaded the development of an online early childhood teacher residency licensure program. Currently, she leads a study on core competencies for early childhood program leaders. Dr. Wen serves on the editorial boards of Early Childhood Research Quarterly and Early Education & Development.